ILLUSTRATED ENCYCLOPEDIA

THE COOK'S GUIDE TO

ASIAN
INGREDIENTS

ILLUSTRATED ENCYCLOPEDIA

THE COOK'S GUIDE TO
ASIAN
INGREDIENTS

SALLIE MORRIS AND DEH-TA HSIUNG

LORENZ BOOKS

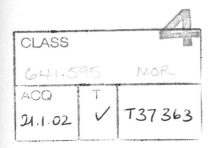
This edition published by Lorenz Books

© Anness Publishing Limited 2000

Lorenz Books is an imprint of
Anness Publishing Limited
Hermes House
88-89 Blackfriars Road
London SE1 8HA

www.lorenzbooks.com

This edition distributed in Canada by Raincoast Books
8680 Cambie Street, Vancouver, British Columbia V6P 6M9

A CIP catalogue record for this book is available from the British Library

PUBLISHER: Joanna Lorenz
EXECUTIVE EDITOR: Linda Fraser
EDITOR: Mariano Kälfors
DESIGNER: Nigel Partridge
PHOTOGRAPHY: Janine Hosegood
FOOD FOR PHOTOGRAPHY: Annabel Ford
EDITORIAL READER: Diane Ashmore

Previously published as part of a larger compendium, *The Practical Encyclopedia of Asian Cooking*

Printed and bound in China

1 3 5 7 9 10 8 6 4 2

NOTES

For all recipes, quantities are given in both metric and imperial measures and, where appropriate, measures are
also given in standard cups and spoons. Follow one set, but not a mixture, because they are not interchangeable.

Standard spoon and cup measures are level.
1 tsp = 5ml, 1 tbsp = 15ml, 1 cup = 250ml/8fl oz

Australian standard tablespoons are 20ml. Australian readers should use 3 tsp
in place of1 tbsp for measuring small quantities of gelatine, cornflour, salt, etc.

Medium eggs are used unless otherwise stated.

CONTENTS

INTRODUCTION

Everything you ever wanted to know about foods from the
Far East and South-east Asia is contained within this
fascinating book, with essential information on hundreds of
ingredients from every part of the region.

Some of the world's most exciting cuisines come from the Far East and South-east Asia. From the vastness of China to the island states of Indonesia and the Philippines, food is prepared with pleasure and keen attention to detail. Each of the countries in this broad sweep has its own unique style of cooking, coloured by climate, local crops, cultural mores and the impact of historical events such as invasion or war, but there are common threads too. Throughout this region, the emphasis is always on serving food that is as fresh as possible. Presentation is paramount, particularly in Japan and Thailand, and the sharing of food is so fundamental to the faith of each culture that honoured guests are precisely that.

Rice is the staple food of the whole of this region. Cultivated in southern Asia for over five thousand years, it is eaten at every meal, including breakfast, and is the basis of both sweet

Above: A variety of crops and grains are grown on the terraced fields on river banks in southern China.

Below: A chef preparing a variety of fresh fish, meats, vegetables and herbs at a roadside food stall in Hong Kong.

and savoury snack foods, as well as being a source for both wine and vinegar. In Japan, vinegared rice is used to make sushi, those delicious titbits that consist either of shaped rice topped with fish or vegetables, or rice and other ingredients rolled in thin sheets of edible seaweed.

Fish forms an important part of the diet. Every country, with the exception of Laos, has miles of coastline, as well as rivers, lakes and ponds, all of which yield plentiful supplies of fish. The lower reaches of the Yangtze River are traditionally known as the "Land of Fish and Rice", a term that is used to indicate the well-being of the local inhabitants. The first king of Siam expressed similar sentiments when, in 1292, he wrote of the value of having "fish in the water and rice in the field".

The Japanese cooks' skill in preparing and serving fish is legendary. This is partly due to the fact that the country has abundant fish stocks and only limited land for grazing, but is also because for many years, meat was off the menu, due to a government decree that prohibited its consumption by any but the sick, on the grounds that it

increased aggression. As a result, Japanese cooks became extremely adept at preparing fish in a wide variety of ways. Very fresh fish is sliced thinly and served raw, or marinated, but this is by no means the only way of preparing it. Fish is also poached, grilled, cooked on skewers and battered and fried in the famous tempura.

In Thailand, too, fish is of enormous importance. As elsewhere in Asia, it is always served as fresh as possible. In restaurants it is usual for diners to

Above: Planting rice in a paddy field in the Mekong Delta, Vietnam. Two crops are harvested each year.

choose their own fish from tanks, a serious business that demands considerable deliberation, and nobody objects to waiting while the grouper or snapper is despatched, prepared and cooked in the manner the host has selected. Fish bought at market is often live and is carried home in a bucket of water for preparation by the cook.

The Asian preoccupation with the freshest possible food, be it animal or vegetable, can be a little disconcerting for the Western visitor. Before enjoying the famous Hong Kong dish Drunken Prawns, for instance, the diner must first watch as the live prawns are marinated in Shao Xing rice wine, then cooked in fragrant stock.

At the other end of the spectrum, salted and cured fish is a valuable source of food throughout the area, but particularly in South-east Asia. All sorts of fish and seafood are prepared in this way, either in brine or by being dried in the sun. Dried fish and shellfish also furnish the raw material for fish sauce and shrimp paste, essential ingredients that go under various names, and contribute a subtle but unique signature to so many dishes.

Below: Fresh red chillies, which are used in many South-east Asian dishes, being sold at a market in Myanmar.

Fish sauce is not the only condiment to play a seminal role in Asian cooking. Even more important is soy sauce, which was invented by the Chinese thousands of years ago. Beancurd (tofu) is another soya bean product that was originally peculiar to the region, but is now widely used in the Western world, as are noodles, another valuable food.

As well as having many ingredients in common, the countries of the Far East and South-east Asia share a similar approach to food. All prepare, cook and serve their daily meals according to the long-established principle the Chinese call *fan-cai*. The "fan" is the main part of the meal, usually rice or another form of grain, while the "cai" includes the supplementary dishes such as fish, meat, poultry and vegetables. These elements must be balanced in every meal, as must the ingredients in

Above: The colourful floating market in Bangkok, Thailand, sells a wonderful selection of fresh fruits and vegetables.

every supplementary dish, so that aromas, colours, textures and tastes are all in perfect harmony.

Harmony dictates that all the dishes be served together, buffet style, rather than as separate courses. Guests begin by taking a portion of rice, and then one

beautifully served. Thai girls learn the art of fruit carving from a young age, and fruit (and vegetables) are cut into fabulous shapes of birds, flowers and butterflies. They are, of course, fortunate in having such wonderful raw materials. Visit the floating market in Bangkok – or, indeed, any market in this part of the world – and you will marvel at the array of vegetables and fruit on offer, many of them relatively unknown in the West until recently, when Asia became such a sought-after travel destination.

Tourism is one of the major reasons why Asian food has become so popular in Europe, America, Australia and elsewhere. Travellers discovered that Chinese food was not a single cuisine, but many, ranging from Peking cooking

Below: Asia is a vast region, from China, through Japan and Korea, down to the South-east Asian islands of Malaysia, Indonesia and the Philippines.

in the north, to the hot and spicy Sichuan-style in the west and Cantonese in the south. Visitors to Vietnam and Thailand learned to enjoy – and distinguish between – the cuisines of those countries and, when they returned home, they wanted to be able to continue eating the meals that had been so much a part of their holiday. In major cities the world over, it is now possible to enjoy authentic Thai, Vietnamese, Indonesian, Malayan and even Filipino food, and it is only a matter of time before lesser-known cuisines are equally well represented.

Home cooks are eager to experiment with this quick, healthy and sensual style of cooking too. Ingredients such as lemon grass and galangal, which could once be bought only in oriental stores are now readily available in many supermarkets. There's never been a better time to discover or extend your repertoire of Asian recipes, and this book is the very best place to start.

of the supplementary dishes on offer, relishing it on its own before taking another portion of rice and a second choice. Soup is served at the same time as other dishes, and is enjoyed throughout the meal.

Harmony extends to presentation, too, an art which reaches its apogee in Japan, where food is valued as much for its aesthetic appearance as for its flavour. In Thailand, too, food is

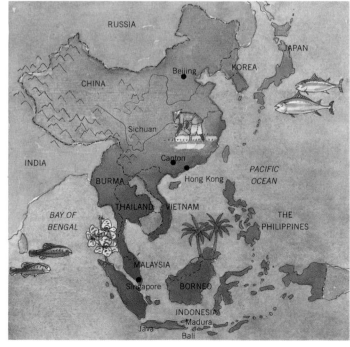

EQUIPMENT AND UTENSILS

The equipment in the average Western kitchen will be perfectly adequate for most of the recipes in this book, particularly now that the wok has become an indispensable item in many households. There are some items, however, that will make cooking Asian food easier and more pleasurable. The fact that many of these simple pieces of equipment also look good, and instantly establish you as an adventurous cook in the eyes of your friends is a bonus.

The best way to build up your store of specialist items is to start slowly, with a few basics such as a cleaver, bamboo steamer and wok, then gradually add extra pieces as you experiment with the exciting and different styles of cooking that are explored within these pages. If you enjoy making sushi, for instance, you will need a mat for rolling, and moulds for shaping the rice; if Thai curries are your current favourite, you'll be glad of a rough mortar and a pestle for grinding wet spice mixtures.

Visit an Asian or Chinese store and you'll be amazed at the array of items on sale at very reasonable prices. The design of many utensils has not changed in centuries, and items made from basic materials are often more effective than modern equivalents.

Cleaver

To Western cooks, a cleaver can seem rather intimidating. In reality, cleavers are among the most useful pieces of equipment ever invented. The blade of a heavy cleaver is powerful enough to cut through bone, yet delicate enough in the hands of a master chef to create paper thin slices of raw fish for sushi. The flat of the broad blade is ideal for crushing garlic or ginger, and the same blade can be used to convey the crushed items to the wok or pan.

Cleavers come in several sizes and weights. Number one is the heaviest. The blade is about 23cm/9in long and 10cm/4in wide. It can weigh as much as 1kg/2¼lb and resembles a chopper more than a knife. At the other end of

the scale, number three has a shorter, narrower blade and is only half as heavy as the larger cleaver. It is mainly used for slicing, rather than chopping. Number two is the cook's favourite. This medium-weight cleaver is used for both slicing and chopping. The Chinese name translates

Above: A medium-weight cleaver is a multi-purpose tool.

as "civil and military knife" because the lighter, front half of the blade is used for slicing, shredding, filleting and scoring (civil work), while the heavier rear half is used for chopping with force (military work). The back of the blade is used for pounding and tenderizing, and the flat for crushing and transporting. Even the handle has more than one purpose – the end can be used as a pestle.

Cleavers are made of several types of material. They can be made of carbonized steel with wooden handles, or of stainless steel with metal or wooden handles. Choose the one you are comfortable with. Hold it in your hand and feel the weight; it should be neither too heavy nor too light. One point to remember is that while a stainless steel cleaver may look good, it will require frequent sharpening if it is to stay razor-sharp. To prevent a carbonized steel blade from rusting and getting stained, wipe it dry after every use, then give it a thin coating of vegetable oil. Cleavers should always be sharpened on a fine-grained whetstone, never with a steel sharpener. The cleaver is user-friendly. It is not as

dangerous as it looks, provided you handle it with care. Learn to regard it as just another kitchen knife, and you will be rewarded with a lot of fun and very satisfactory results.

Chopping block

The traditional chopping block in the East is simply a cross-section of a tree trunk, usually hardwood. The ideal size for use in a domestic kitchen is about 30cm/12in in diameter and about 5cm/2in thick, but you will see much larger blocks being used in restaurants.

Season a new block with a liberal dose of vegetable oil on both sides to prevent it from splitting. Let it absorb as much oil as it will take, then clean the block with salt and water and dry it thoroughly. After each use, scrape the surface with the back of your cleaver, then wipe it down with a cloth. Never immerse a wooden block in water.

A large rectangular cutting board of hardwood can be used instead, but make sure it is at least 5cm/2in thick or it may not be able to take a hard blow from a cleaver. Acrylic boards can obviously be used if preferred, but they will not have the same aesthetic appeal as a traditional wooden one.

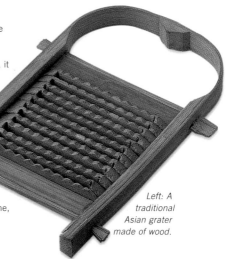

Left: A traditional Asian grater made of wood.

Above: The rough surface of a stone mortar and pestle helps grip the ingredients that are being pounded.

Grater

Traditional graters, used for preparing ginger, galangal and daikon (mooli), are made from wood or bamboo, but a metal cheese grater makes a satisfactory substitute.

Mortar and pestle

Oriental cooks prefer granite or stone mortars and pestles, since these have rough surfaces which help to grip the ingredients that are being chopped or pounded. Bigger, flat-bowled mortars are good for making spice pastes that contain large amounts of fresh spices, onion, herbs and garlic.

Spice mill

If you are going to grind a lot of spices, a spice mill will prove useful. An electric coffee grinder works well for this purpose,

Right: A double-handled wok is useful for all types of cooking; those with a single handle are particularly good for stir-frying.

but it is a good idea to reserve the mill for spices, unless you like to have your coffee flavoured with cardamom or cloves.

Wok

It is not surprising that the wok has become a universal favourite, for it is a remarkably versatile utensil. The rounded bottom was originally designed to fit snugly on a traditional Chinese brazier or stove. It conducts and retains heat evenly and because of its shape, the food always returns to the centre where the heat is most intense. This makes it ideally suited for stir-frying, braising, steaming, boiling and even for deep-frying.

Although the wok might not at first glance appear to be the best utensil for deep-frying, it is actually ideal, requiring far less oil than a flat-bottomed deep-fryer. It has more depth and a greater frying surface, so more food can be cooked more quickly. It is also much safer than a saucepan. As a wok has a larger capacity at the top than at the base, there is plenty of room to

accommodate the oil, even when extra ingredients are added, and it is not likely to overflow and catch fire.

There are two basic types of wok available in the West. The most common type, the double handled wok, is suitable for all types of cooking. The single-handled wok is particularly suitable for quick stir-frying, as it can easily be shaken during cooking. Both types are available with flattened bases for use on electric cookers or gas cookers with burners that would not accommodate a round base.

The best woks are made from lightweight carbonized steel. Cast iron woks are too heavy for all but the strongest cooks to handle, and woks made from other materials, such as stainless steel or aluminium, are not as good for Asian cooking. They also tend to be a great deal more expensive than the standard carbonized steel wok.

A new carbonized steel wok must be seasoned before use. The best way to do this is to place the wok over a high heat until the surface blackens, then wash it in warm, soapy water. Use a stiff brush to get the wok clean, then rinse it well in clean water and place it over a medium heat to dry completely. Finally, wipe the surface with a pad of kitchen paper soaked in vegetable oil. After each use, wash the wok under the hot water tap, but never use detergent as this would remove the "seasoning" and cause the wok to rust. Any food that sticks to the wok should be scraped off with a stiff brush or with a non-metal scourer, and the wok should then be rinsed and dried over a low heat. Before being put away, a little oil should be rubbed in to the surface of the wok.

Below right: A perforated metal scoop and a wire skimmer

Above: Essential wok tools include a dome-shaped lid, wooden or bamboo chopsticks, a long-handled spatula and a large ladle.

Wok tools

Some wok sets come with a spatula and ladle made from cast iron or stainless steel. These are very useful, particularly the ladle. It addition to its obvious purpose as a stirrer, it can be used to measure small quantities of liquid. A standard ladle holds about 175ml/ 6fl oz/¾ cup. A dome-shaped lid is also useful, as is a metal draining rack that fits over the wok. Small items such as deep-fried foods can be placed on the rack to keep warm while successive batches are cooked. Other accessories include wooden or bamboo chopsticks. Short ones can be used at the table or in the kitchen – they are ideal for beating eggs – and the long pair are used for deep-frying, as stirrers or tongs. Finally, a wok stand is handy for protecting your table when serving.

Strainers

Several types of strainer are available, but the two most useful are the perforated metal scoop or slotted spoon, and the coarse-mesh, wire skimmer, preferably with a long bamboo handle. Wire skimmers come in a variety of sizes and are useful for removing food from hot oil when deep-frying.

Below: Bamboo steamers come in several sizes.

Steamers

The traditional Chinese steamer is made from bamboo and has a tight-fitting lid. Several sizes are available, and you can stack as many tiers as you like over a wok of boiling water. The modern steamer is free-standing and made of aluminium, but the food cooked in a metal steamer lacks the subtle fragrance that a bamboo steamer imparts. If you do not have a steamer, you can improvise with a wok and a trivet. Having placed the trivet in the wok, fill it one-third full of water

Above: An authentic clay pot can be used in the oven or, with care, on top of the stove.

and bring this to the boil. Place the food in a heatproof bowl on the trivet, cover the wok with the dome-shaped lid and steam the food until it is cooked.

Clay pot

Also known as the sand-pot or Chinese casserole, this earthenware cooking utensil must have preceded the cast iron pot by thousands of years. Several shapes and sizes are available, and most are glazed on the inside only. They are not expensive and can be bought in

Below: A large saucepan with a tight-fitting lid is ideal for cooking rice.

Asian or Chinese stores. With care, the pots can be used on top of the stove, where they retain an even heat. They are, however, fairly fragile, and are prone to crack easily.

Rice cooker

Electric rice cookers work extremely well and are worth investing in if you cook a lot of rice. However, a good-sized, deep, heavy-based saucepan with a tight-fitting lid is just as suitable for this purpose.

Mongolian fire pot

Also known as a Chinese hot pot or steamboat (in Singapore), this is not unlike a fondue pot, in that it allows food to be cooked at the table. The design is different from that of a fondue, however, as it consists of a central funnel, which is filled with burning charcoal, surrounded by a moat in which hot stock is placed. The pot is placed in the centre of the table and guests cook small pieces of meat and vegetables in the hot stock. Once these are all cooked and eaten, the stock is served as a soup. There are several different models available, the most expensive being made of brass, while the cheaper ones are made of aluminium or stainless steel.

Japanese omelette pan

To make the rolled omelettes that are so widely used in Japanese cooking, a rectangular omelette pan or *makiyaki-nabe* is useful, but not essential: a large non-stick, heavy-based frying pan or a flat, heavy griddle could be used instead.

Below: A Mongolian fire pot or steamboat is used for cooking at the table. The central funnel is filled with burning charcoal, and this heats the stock in the surrounding moat.

Sushi equipment

If you are going to make sushi properly, you will need a few simple pieces of equipment. A *makisu*, also known as a *sushimaki sudare*, is essential. This is the bamboo mat (shown below), which is about the size of a table mat, that is used for rolling sheets of nori (seaweed) around vinegared rice and other fillings when making *norimaki*.

Sushi chefs spread the rice on the nori with their fingers, but this is a sticky business and can prove tricky for the uninitiated. A rice paddle or *shamoji* makes the job easier. For pressed sushi, shaped moulds made from wood or plastic are very useful.

INGREDIENTS

This visual catalogue includes essential information on every type of Asian food, from the daily staples, such as rice and noodles, to unusual fruit and vegetables and exotic fish, and includes preparation, cooking and storing instructions.

RICE

CHINESE: *MI;* THAI: *KHAO*

Rice is the staple grain of the whole of Asia, which is well over half the world's population. It is true that wheat is also grown in northern China and India, but its consumption is rather small in comparison with rice.

Throughout Asia, the importance of rice is underlined by the fact that in Chinese and other Asian languages, there is no single word for rice, but many. The crop, grain, raw rice and cooked rice are all referred to by different terms, and the Chinese character *fan* for cooked rice has acquired a much wider meaning in colloquial speech; it is also synonymous with nourishment and good health. When friends meet, instead of asking "How do you do?" they will often greet each other with the words: "Have you eaten rice?" An affirmative answer indicates that all is well.

Another common Chinese word with more than one meaning is *fan-wan* (rice-bowl). Aside from the obvious, this also means a job or livelihood; so the expression "to lose one's rice bowl" or "to have one's rice bowl broken", suggests that one has been given the sack; similarly, someone described as having an "iron rice-bowl" has probably got a job for life. Paradoxically, the expression *fan-tong,* which means a rice bucket (something that holds a large amount of cooked rice) has become a derogatory expression to describe a person who lacks refinement (a big eater of plain rice).

Rice has been cultivated in southern Asia for over five thousand years. There are more than forty thousand different strains grown in China alone. Since rice requires a wet and warm climate for its cultivation, some 90 per cent of the world production of rice is grown (and consumed) in the monsoon regions of Asia. A small amount of rice is cultivated on dry land in northern China, but because of the cold climate, only one crop can be grown each year, whereas two crops per annum is the norm in the temperate south.

Below: Patna rice is one of the many types of long grain rice.

Above: Thai fragrant rice has a delicate, fragrant scent.

Freshly harvested rice has a special aroma, and is eagerly sought after in China and Japan, the rice from the autumn harvest (usually in November) being reckoned to taste the best.

TYPES OF RICE

Broadly speaking, rice can be classified as being either *Oryza sativa indica* or *Oryza sativa japonica.* Varieties of both types are cultivated in Asia. Long grained indica *(xian)* rices – of which there are many strains – are the most common. Long grain white rice has had its husk, bran and germ removed, taking most of the nutrients with them and leaving a bland-flavoured rice that is light and fluffy when cooked. Long grain brown rice has had only its outer husk removed, leaving the bran and germ intact, which gives it a chewy, nutty flavour. It takes longer to cook than white rice but contains more fibre, vitamins and minerals.

Patna rice gets its name from Patna in India. At one time, most of the long grain rice sold in Europe came from Patna, and the term was used loosely to mean any long grain rice. The custom

persists in parts of America, but elsewhere Patna is used to describe a variety of long grain rice from the Bihar region of India.

Basmati rice is a slender long grain rice that is grown in northern India, in the Punjab, in parts of Pakistan and in the foothills of the Himalayas. After harvesting it is aged for a year, which gives it a characteristic flavour and a light, fluffy texture. The grains are long and slender, and become even longer during cooking. Widely used in Indian cooking, basmati rice has a cooling effect on hot and spicy curries.

Thai fragrant rice has a delicate but distinctive scent of jasmine, and is particularly highly prized.

Short-grained japonica *(geng)* rices are less fragrant, but tend to taste slightly sweeter than indicas. This type of rice is cultivated in northern China, Japan, Korea and surrounding areas. The rices are higher in amylopectin than long grains, and are therefore more starchy. The grains cling together when cooked, which makes them ideal for sushi and similar Japanese dishes.

Glutinous rice – also known as sweet or waxy rice – is even more sticky than Japanese short grain rice. This endears it to South-east Asian cooks, as the cooked rice can be shaped or rolled, and is very easy to pick up with chopsticks. White glutinous rice, with its fat, opaque grains, is the most common type, but there is also a black glutinous rice, which retains the husk and has a nutty flavour. A pinkish-red glutinous rice is cultivated on the banks of the Yangtze River, and a purple black variety has recently been developed. Glutinous rice has a high sugar content, and is used in Japan for making *senbei* (rice crackers) and *mochi* (rice cakes), as well as sweet rice wine.

Right: Short-grained japonica rice is ideal for sushi because, when cooked, the grains stick together.

Above: Basmati rice is considered by many people to be the prince of rice. There are various grades of basmati, but it is impossible to differentiate between them except by trying various brands to discover the best fragrance and taste.

Culinary uses

It is impossible to think of Asian food without rice. Rice is served in one form or another at every meal, including breakfast. Although wheat – in the form of dumplings or noodles – is eaten more often than rice in some parts of Asia, such as northern China, Asians everywhere regard rice as their staple food, with wheaten foods as mere supplements. In some languages the phrase for eating rice is the same as that for eating food.

The most common way of serving rice throughout Asia is simply boiled or steamed; fried rice does not normally form part of an everyday meal, but is either served as a snack on its own, or reserved for a special occasion such as a banquet. Unlike the India pilau, the Italian risotto or the Spanish paella, Asian fried rice dishes are never based upon raw rice, but always use ready cooked rice (either boiled or steamed). For the finest results, the rice should be cold and firm, rather than soft.

The universal breakfast in all Asian countries is a creamy, moist rice dish, which is known as congee or rice pudding. Considered to be highly nutritious, it is often given to babies and people with digestive problems as well as the elderly. Coconut milk is used instead of water in many South-east Asian countries, but because it usually takes over an hour to make a smooth, creamy congee, many Japanese cooks (and some Chinese) cheat by simply adding hot water to cold cooked rice.

Below: Black and white glutinous rice

others, and the amount of liquid required varies, too. The general rule is to use double the amount of water by volume to dry rice. However, if the rice has been washed or soaked first, less water will be needed otherwise, when cooked, the rice will be soft and sticky, instead of firm and fluffy.

Asian cooks often add a teaspoon of vegetable oil to the water to prevent the rice from sticking to the bottom of the pan. Whether to add salt or not is a matter of choice. It is usually added when cooking regular long grain rice, but not for Thai fragrant rice. The width, depth and material of the pan used will also make a difference to the result. One of the best ways of cooking perfect boiled rice is in an electric rice-cooker, while some cooks get very good results in the microwave.

Storage

Raw rice should not be kept for too long, or the grains will lose their fragrance. Keep the rice in an airtight container in a dry, cool place, away from strong light, and use it within 3–4 months of purchasing.

Preparation and cooking techniques

There can never be a definitive recipe for cooking plain rice, because each type requires individual treatment.

Some benefit from being rinsed in cold water first, while others should be soaked before use. Some types of rice need to be cooked for longer than

---

Plain boiled rice
Use long grain Patna or basmati rice; or better still, try Thai fragrant rice. Allow 50g/2oz/generous ¼ cup raw rice per person.

1 Put the dry rice in a colander and rinse it under cold running water.

2 Tip into a large pan, then pour in enough cold water to come 2cm/¾in above the surface of rice. (In Asia the traditional way of measuring this is with the help of the index finger. When the tip of the finger is touching the surface of the rice, the water level should just reach the first joint.)

3 Add a pinch of salt, and, if you like, about 5ml/1 tsp vegetable oil, stir once and bring to the boil.

4 Stir once more, reduce the heat to the lowest possible setting and cover the pan with a tight-fitting lid.

5 Cook for 12–15 minutes, then turn off the heat and leave the rice to stand, tightly covered, for about 10 minutes. Fluff up the rice with a fork before serving.

FLOURS

The most popular thickening agents in Asian cooking are cornflour, tapioca flour and potato flour. Mung bean flour, water chestnut flour, lotus root and arrowroot are favoured for clear sauces. Chick-pea flour is used to make batters. Rice flour is used as a thickener, and for rice papers, dumplings and cakes.

Cornflour

This fine white powder, made from corn (maize) is a useful thickening agent for sauces, soups and casseroles.

Rice flour

More finely milled than ground rice, this is also known as rice powder. The texture is similar to that of cornflour. Rice flour is used for thickening sauces, and to make rice papers and the dough for dumplings. It is often used to make sticky Asian cakes and sweets, but because rice flour does not contain gluten, the cakes made with it are rather flat. Rice flour can be combined with wheat flour to make bread, but this produces a crumbly loaf.

Chick-pea flour

This very fine flour is also called gram flour, or besan. Mainly used in India, where it originated, it also plays a role in Malayan cooking, thanks to Indian immigrants who introduced it.

Wheat flour

Ground from the whole grain, this may be wholemeal or white. Hard, or strong wheat flour is high in gluten, which makes it ideal for adding to rice flour to make bread.

Soya flour

This is a finely-ground, high-protein flour made from the soya bean. It is used as a thickener in a wide range of sauces and soups, and is often mixed with other flours such as wheat flour to make bread and pastries. It adds a pleasant nutty flavour.

Left: Japanese rice flour

Far left: Japanese wheat flour

Below: Chick-pea flour

Left: Thai rice flour

Right: Cornflour

Left: Japanese soya flour

NOODLES

Whether Marco Polo actually introduced noodles from China to Italy is a debatable point, but we do know that noodles made from wheat flour appeared in China as early as the first century BC, around the time of the Roman Empire. Noodles rapidly became a popular food, not only in China, but throughout the whole of Asia.

Up to the end of the last century, when modern machinery was first imported from Europe, noodles were always made by hand, and even today, certain types of noodle are still hand-made, most notably, the "hand-pulled" or "drawn" noodles made by chefs in northern China. It takes more than ten years to master the technique, so is beyond the reach of ordinary mortals.

Noodles form an important part of the daily diet in the Far East, ranking second only to rice as a staple food. Unlike rice and steamed buns, however, which are usually served plain to be eaten with cooked dishes, noodles are

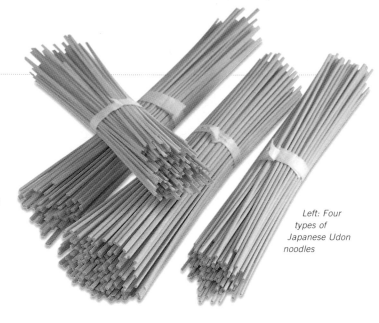

Left: Four types of Japanese Udon noodles

Below: Plain Chinese (top) and Thai noodles (bottom)

usually cooked with other ingredients. For this reason, noodle dishes are seldom served as accompaniments, but are eaten on their own as light meals or snacks. In Vietnam, rice noodle soup is the standard breakfast. In Japan there are restaurants that specialize in noodle dishes such as noodles served solo with dipping sauces; bowls of steaming noodle soup; and noodles cooked with slivered vegetables and seaweed.

Below: Bundles of thin, white, Japanese Somen noodles

Thailand has its noodle stalls, noodle boats and even noodle meals on wheels available from vendors with ingenious mobile shops mounted on their bicycles. In Asia, you need never be far from a noodle seller.

WHEAT NOODLES

Asian noodles are made from a variety of flour pastes, including wheat, rice, mung bean, buckwheat, seaweed, corn and even devil's tongue, which is a plant related to the arum lily. Some noodles are plain, others are enriched with egg. Dried wheat noodles, with or without eggs, are often called "longevity noodles" because of their association with long life.

Right: Fresh egg noodles

Plain noodles
Made from strong plain wheat flour and water, these can be flat or round and come in various thicknesses. In Japan, they are known as **Udon** and are available fresh, pre-cooked or dried. **Somen** are thin, delicate, white Japanese noodles. They are sold in bundles, held in place by a paper band.

Egg noodles These are far more common than plain wheat noodles. In China they come in various thicknesses and are sold fresh or dried. **Ramen** are the Japanese equivalent and are usually sold in coils or blocks. Very fine egg noodles, which resemble vermicelli, are called **Yi noodles** in China, after the family that originally made them. They are popular in Hakka-style cooking.

Shrimp noodles These seasoned egg noodles are flavoured with fresh shrimp and/or shrimp roe, They are usually sold dried, in coils of various widths.

Instant noodles Packets of pre-cooked egg noodles are a familiar sight in the West. They come in various flavourings, such as chicken, prawn and beef.

Preparation and cooking techniques

Noodles are very easy to prepare. Some types benefit from being soaked before being cooked, so see individual recipes for advice, read the instructions on the packet or seek advice from someone in the store where you bought them. Both dried and fresh noodles have to be cooked in boiling water before use. How long for depends on the type of noodle, the thickness of the strips, and whether (as is usual) the noodles will be cooked again in a soup or sauce. Dried noodles generally require about 3 minutes' cooking, while fresh ones will often be ready in less than a minute, and may need to be rinsed under cold water to prevent them from overcooking.

After the initial cooking, noodles are then usually prepared and served in one of the following ways:

Noodles in soup
Most popular in China, Korea, Japan, Vietnam, Burma and Singapore, this usually consists of noodles served in bowls of clear broth with pieces of cooked meat, poultry, seafood and/or vegetables, sometimes with a sharp sauce on the side.

Braised noodles *(lao mein)*
The difference between this and noodles in soup is that braised noodles are first cooked in a broth, then served with a thickened sauce.

Fried noodles
(chow mein) This has to be one of the most popular Chinese dishes in the West (and in South-east Asia, but not so much in north China or Japan). The two basic types of fried noodles are dry-fried (crisp) or soft-fried. Generally speaking, only the fine vermicelli-type of noodles are used for dry-frying; the thicker round or flat noodles are more suitable for soft-frying.

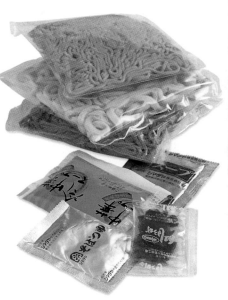

Left: Blocks of dried Japanese Ramen noodles

Above: Instant noodles come in a variety of flavourings.

RICE NOODLES

CHINESE: *MIFEN;* VIETNAMESE: *LAI FAN*

Wheat noodles must have preceded rice noodles by several centuries, since there were no written records of their existence until well into the Han Dynasty in the third century AD. Not surprisingly, rice noodles are very popular in southern China and South-east Asia where not much wheat is grown.

Unlike most other noodles, which are made from flour of one type or another, rice noodles are made from whole grains of rice, which are soaked and then ground with water into a paste. This paste is drained through a sieve to form a dough, which is divided into two. One half is cooked in boiling water for

Below: Thin and thick Chinese rice noodles or sticks

Above: Fine Thai rice noodles are sometimes referred to as vermicelli.

15 minutes, before it is kneaded with the raw half to make a firm dough. The dough is then put through a press, which cuts it into various shapes and sizes. The finished strands are blanched in water, drained and rinsed before being sold as fresh noodles, or dried in the sun before packaging.

Types of rice noodles

Although they are known by different names, the rice noodles sold in southern China, Thailand and Vietnam are all similar. Like wheat noodles, they come in various widths, from the very thin strands known as rice vermicelli or *lai fan* (*sen mee* in Thailand) to rice sticks, which start at around 2mm/1⁄16in and can be as wide as 1cm/1⁄2in, as in the case of *ho fun,* a special variety from south China reputedly made with river water rather than tap water. In Thailand it is possible to buy a rice noodle enriched with egg. Called *ba mee,* it is sold in nests. A wide range of dried rice noodles is available in Asian or Chinese stores, and fresh ones can occasionally be found in the chiller cabinets.

Preparation and cooking techniques

Because all rice noodles are pre-cooked, they need only be soaked in hot water for a few minutes to soften them before use. If they are soaked for too long, they will go soggy and lose the texture that is part of their appeal.

Below: Japanese rice noodles

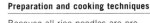

Preparing rice noodles

Rice noodles need only to be soaked in hot water for a few minutes to soften them.

Add the noodles to a large bowl of water that has been recently boiled and leave for 5–10 minutes, or until softened, stirring occasionally to separate the strands as they soften.

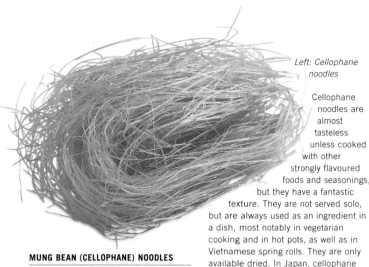

MUNG BEAN (CELLOPHANE) NOODLES

CHINESE: *FENSI*; VIETNAMESE: *BUN*;
JAPANESE: *HARUSAME*

Also known as transparent noodles, bean thread vermicelli or glass noodles, these very fine, rather brittle strands are made from green mung beans, which are the same beans as those used for sprouting. Although very thin, the strands are firm and resilient, and they stay that way when cooked, never becoming soggy, which doubtless contributes to their popularity.

Preparing cellophane noodles
Cellophane noodles are never served on their own, but always used as an ingredient in a dish. Soak them in hot or warm water for 10–15 minutes to soften them.

When they are soft, use a pair of scissors or a sharp knife to chop the noodles into shorter strands for easier handling.

Left: Cellophane noodles

Cellophane noodles are almost tasteless unless cooked with other strongly flavoured foods and seasonings, but they have a fantastic texture. They are not served solo, but are always used as an ingredient in a dish, most notably in vegetarian cooking and in hot pots, as well as in Vietnamese spring rolls. They are only available dried. In Japan, cellophane noodles are called *harusame*, which means "spring rain".

BUCKWHEAT NOODLES

JAPANESE: *SOBA*

The best-known buckwheat noodles are the Japanese soba, which are usually sold dried in bundles of fine strands. Soba are much darker in colour than wheat noodles. There is also a dark green variety called cha-soba (tea soba), which is made of buckwheat and green tea. Korean cooks use buckwheat noodles, too, preferring a very thin variety.

Unusual noodles

Shirataki This popular Japanese noodle (*above left*) is made from a starch derived from the tubers of the devil's tongue plant, which is related to the arum lily.
Bijon Made from corn, these noodles (*above right*) are made in South-east Asia.
Canton These Chinese wheat noodles are sometimes enriched with eggs (*above top*).

Storage

Packets of fresh noodles normally carry a use-by date, and must, of course, be stored in the fridge. Dried noodles will keep for many months if kept sealed in the original packet, or in airtight containers in a cool, dry place, but again, the packets have an expiry date.

Below: Soba noodles

PANCAKES AND WRAPPERS

PANCAKES

CHINESE: *BING*

The pancakes of Asia are quite different from their counterparts in the West. For a start, they are almost always made from plain dough, rather than a batter, and they are more often than not served with savoury fillings rather than sweet.

There are two types of pancakes in China, either thin or thick. Thin pancakes *(bobing)* are also known as mandarin or duck pancakes, because they are used as wrappers for serving the famous Peking duck. They are also served with other savoury dishes, most notably, the very popular *mu-shu* or *moo-soo* pork, which consists of scrambled egg with pork and wood ears

(dried black fungus). Making pancakes demands considerable dexterity, so many cooks prefer to buy them frozen from the Chinese supermarket.

Thick pancakes are made with lard and flavoured with savoury ingredients such as spring onions and rock salt. In northern China, they are eaten as a snack, or as part of a main meal, rather like the Indian paratha. Both thin and thick pancakes are sometimes served as a dessert, with a filling of sweetened bean paste.

NONYA SPRING ROLL PANCAKES

These are the exception to the rule that most pancakes in the East are made from dough. Typical of the Singaporean style of cooking known as Nonya, they

are made from an egg, flour and cornflour batter and are traditionally served with a wide selection of fillings.

Reheating Chinese pancakes

1 Stack the pancakes, interleaving them with squares of non-stick baking paper.

2 Carefully wrap the stacked pancakes in foil, folding over the sides of the foil so that the pancakes are completely sealed.

3 Put the foil parcel in a steamer and cover. Place the steamer on a trivet in a wok of simmering water. Steam for 3–5 minutes until the pancakes are hot.

Above: Thick pancakes are eaten as a savoury snack, or filled with sweet bean paste and served as a dessert.

Below: Thin pancakes are used as wrappers, notably for Peking duck, or served with savoury dishes.

SPRING ROLL WRAPPERS

MANDARIN: *CHUNJUAN PI;* CANTONESE: *SHUEN GUEN PIE*

Spring rolls are called egg rolls in the USA, and pancake rolls in many other parts of the world. They must be one of the most popular Chinese snacks everywhere, including China itself. While the fillings may vary from region to region, or even between different restaurants and fast food stalls, the wrappers are always more or less the same. They are made from a simple flour and water dough, except in Vietnam, where wrappers are made from rice flour, water and salt.

There are three different sizes of ready-made spring roll wrappers available from the freezers of Asian stores: small, medium and large. They are all wafer-thin. The smallest wrappers, which are about 12cm/4½ in square, are used for making dainty, cocktail-style rolls. The standard-size

wrappers measure 21–23cm/8½–9in square, and usually come in packets of 20 sheets. The largest, 30cm/12in square, are too big for general use, so they are usually cut in half or into strips for making samosas and similar snacks.

Above: Small and medium-size spring roll wrappers. Any unused wrappers can be returned to the freezer.

Preparing spring rolls

Use medium-size spring roll wrappers, which you will find in the freezer cabinet in Asian or Chinese stores. They should be thawed before use. For the filling, use ingredients such as beansprouts, bamboo shoots, water chestnuts and dried mushrooms, with chopped prawns or finely minced pork. When you have prepared the rolls, deep-fry them a few at a time in hot oil for 2–3 minutes, or until golden and crisp.

2 Spoon the spring roll filling diagonally across the wrapper.

4 Brush the edges of the wrapper with a little cornflour and water paste.

1 Peel off the top spring roll wrapper. Cover the rest to keep them moist.

3 Fold over the nearest corner of the wrapper to cover the filling.

5 Fold the edges towards the middle, then roll up in to a neat parcel.

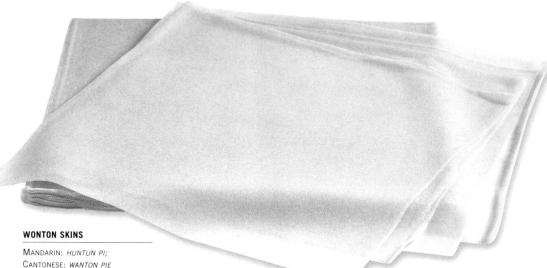

WONTON SKINS

MANDARIN: *HUNTUN PI;*
CANTONESE: *WANTON PIE*

Wonton skins or wrappers are made from a flour and egg dough, which is rolled out to a smooth, flat thin sheet, as when making egg noodles. The sheet is usually cut into small squares, although round wonton wrappers are also available. Ready-made wonton skins are stacked in piles of 25 or 50, wrapped and sold fresh or frozen in Asian or Chinese stores.

Unlike spring roll wrappers, which have to be carefully peeled off sheet by sheet before use, fresh wonton skins are dusted with flour before being packed, This keeps each one separate from the others and so they are very easy to use. Frozen wrappers must, however, be thawed thoroughly before use, or they will tend to stick together. Any unused skins can be re-frozen, but should be carefully wrapped in foil so that they do not dry out in the freezer.

There are several ways of using wonton skins. They can be deep-fried and served with a dip, filled and boiled, steamed or deep-fried, or simply poached in a clear broth. On most Chinese restaurant menus in the West, this last option is listed under soups, which is misleading, as in China and South-east Asia, wonton soup is always served solo as a snack, never as a separate soup course as part of a meal.

Above: Large spring roll wrappers can be cut into strips for making samosas.

Below: Wonton skins can be square or round and come in a variety of sizes.

Preparing Wontons

Place the filling in the centre of the wonton skin and dampen the edges. Press the edges of the wonton skin together to create a little purse shape, sealing the filling completely.

RICE PAPERS

VIETNAMESE: *BANH TRANG*

The rice paper used in Vietnamese (and Thai) cooking is quite different from the rice paper that is used for writing and painting in China and Japan, nor does it bear any resemblance to the sheets of rice paper British cooks use as pan liners when baking macaroons. Made from rice flour, water and salt, it is a round, tissue-thin "crepe", dried on bamboo mats in the sun, which results in the familiar crosshatch pattern being embedded on each sheet.

Rice paper is used for wrapping Vietnamese spring rolls and small pieces of meat and fish to be eaten in the hand. The sheets are rather dry and brittle, so must be softened by soaking in warm water for a few seconds before use. Alternatively, they can be placed on damp dish towels and brushed with water until they are sufficiently pliable to be used. Spring rolls are usually deep-fried, but this is not always the case. Vietnamese cooks also make a fresh version. Cooked pork, prawns, beansprouts and vermicelli are wrapped in rice paper, which has been dipped in cold water until it is pliable and transparent. The filling can clearly be seen through the wrappers, and the rolls look very pretty.

Storage

Packaged and sold in 15cm/6in, 25cm/10in and 30cm/12in rounds, rice papers will keep for months in a cool, dry place, provided the packages are tightly sealed. When buying, look for sheets that are of an even thickness, with a clear, whitish colour. Broken pieces are a sign of bad handling, and are quite useless for wrapping, so avoid any packages that look as if they have been knocked about.

Below: Rice papers are dried on bamboo mats, which give them their familiar cross-hatch pattern.

DUMPLINGS

MANDARIN: *JIAO ZI/BAO ZI;* CANTONESE: *DIM SUM*

Dumplings are very popular in China, and there is a wide variety of different shapes and sizes, with fillings ranging from pork and vegetables to mushrooms and bamboo shoots. Some enclose the filling in a very thin dough skin *(jiao zi)* while others use a dough made from a glutinous rice flour. There are also steamed buns *(bao zi)* filled with meat or a sweet bean paste.

The best way to experience the diversity and delicious flavours of dumplings is to indulge in dim sum, that wonderful procession of tasty morsels that the Cantonese have elevated to an art form. Although dumplings originated in northern China, it was in Canton that the practice developed of enjoying these snacks with tea at breakfast or lunch time.

Dim sum literally means "dot on the heart" and indicates a snack or refreshment, not a full blown meal. Although the range of dishes available on a dim sum menu now embraces other specialities (spring rolls, wontons and spare ribs, for instance), dumplings remain the essential items.

Below: Grilled dumplings or "pot stickers" and chilli sauce.

What is more, unlike the majority of dim sum, which are so complicated to make that they can only be prepared by a highly skilled chef, dumplings are comparatively simple to make at home. Both *jiao zi* and *bao zi* are available ready-made from Asian or Chinese stores – the former are sold uncooked and frozen, and the latter are ready-cooked and sold chilled.

Preparation and cooking techniques

Frozen *jiao zi* dumplings should be cooked straight from the freezer. There are three different ways of cooking and serving them.

Poaching

The most common way of cooking dumplings in China is to poach them in boiling water for 4–5 minutes – longer if cooking from frozen.

The dumplings are added to boiling water. When the water boils again, a cupful of cold water is added to the pan and the water is brought to the boil again. This is repeated twice more, by which time the dumplings will be ready. They are traditionally served hot with a vinegar and soy sauce dip, chilli sauce or chilli oil.

Cooking Dumplings

1 To poach dumplings, drop them into boiling water. When the water boils again, add a cupful of cold water. Repeat twice more, cooking the dumplings for 4–5 minutes.

2 To steam dumplings, place them on a bed of lettuce or spinach leaves on the base of a bamboo steamer, cover with the lid and cook for 8–10 minutes.

3 To "grill" dumplings, fry in a shallow frying pan until they are brown, then add a little water, cover with a bamboo steamer lid, and cook until the water has completely evaporated.

Above: Plain steamed buns and sweet buns filled with bean paste.

Steaming

The best way to do this is by using a bamboo basket as a steamer. The dumplings are placed on a bed of lettuce or spinach leaves on the rack of the steamer, which is then covered. The dumplings are served hot with a dip.

Grilling

This description is a bit misleading, because the dumplings are not grilled in the conventional sense but are cooked in a flat frying pan. The dumplings are first shallow-fried, then a small amount of boiling water is added to the pan and they are steamed under cover until all the liquid has evaporated. When cooked by this method, the dumplings are crispy on the base, soft on top and juicy inside. They are often called by their popular name, which is "pot stickers".

PEKING DUMPLINGS

These crescent-shaped dumplings are filled with minced pork, greens and spring onions and seasoned with salt, sugar, soy sauce, rice wine and sesame oil. In northern China they are eaten for breakfast on New Year's Day, but are available all year round, and are often served as snacks or as part of a meal.

STEAMED BUNS

Steamed buns are to Asia what baked bread is to the West, and *bao* (filled buns) are the Chinese fast food equivalent of hot dogs, hamburgers and sandwiches. There are two main types of steamed buns, either plain or filled. The plain, unfilled buns made from leavened dough are treated in much the same way as plain boiled rice and are intended to be eaten with cooked food. Then there are filled buns *(bao zi)*. The name literally means "wraps" and these can be savoury or sweet. The sweet ones usually contain either a lotus seed paste or a sweet bean paste filling and are usually eaten cold. Savoury *bao zi* come with a wide range of fillings, the most common being pork, and a very popular type is filled with Cantonese *char siu* (honey-roasted pork). These are available ready-made, and are best eaten hot.

Also available ready-made, but uncooked, are what are known as Shanghai dumplings. These are little round dumplings, much smaller than *char siu bao*, and each consisting of minced pork wrapped in a thin skin of unleavened dough.

Prawn crackers

Prawn crackers, also called shrimp chips, are made from fresh prawns, starch, salt and sugar. They are very popular as cocktail snacks, and some restaurants serve them while you wait for your order to arrive. The raw crackers are grey in colour. The small Chinese ones are not much bigger than a thumbnail, while those used in Indonesia are much larger, about 15cm/6in long and 5cm/2in wide. Indonesian prawn crackers are more difficult to find in the West. Once deep-fried, both types puff up to four or five times the original size, and become almost snow white. Ready-cooked crackers are also available. They are sold in sealed packets, but do not keep well once exposed to the air, so should be eaten as soon as possible after opening.

VEGETABLES

CHINESE LEAVES

MANDARIN: *DA BAICAI; HUANG YA BAI;*
CANTONESE: *SHAO CHOI; WONG NGA BAK*

There are almost as many names for this member of the brassica family as there are ways of cooking it. In the West, it is generally called Chinese leaves, but it is also known as Chinese cabbage, Napa cabbage (mainly in the USA) or celery cabbage. The alternative Chinese name translates as "yellow-sprouting-white", a description of the crinkled leaves, and the Cantonese call it Peking or Tianjin cabbage in honour of its northern origin.

It is a cool season vegetable, most abundant from November through to April, but available all year round. There are three common varieties which all look similar, but differ in length, width and tightness of leaf.

Aroma and flavour

Chinese leaves have a delicate sweet aroma with a mild cabbage flavour that disappears completely when the vegetable is cooked. The white stalk has a crunchy texture, and it remains succulent even after long cooking.

Culinary uses

This is a very versatile vegetable and it can be used in stir-fries, stews, soups or salads. It will absorb the flavours of any other ingredients with which it is cooked – be they fish or shellfish, poultry, meat or vegetables – and yet retain its own characteristic flavour and texture. In Asian or Chinese restaurants, braised Chinese leaves are often served as a flavoursome base for roasted meats or duck.

Preparation and cooking techniques

Discard the outer layer of leaves and trim off the root, then slice off as much you need. Should you wish to wash the leaves (and this is not strictly necessary unless you are using them in a salad), do so before cutting them, otherwise you will wash away much of the vitamins. If you stir-fry Chinese leaves in hot oil, the stalks often develop dark scorch marks. Restaurant chefs blanch the vegetable in boiling stock, which enhances the flavour, before frying.

Storage

Chinese leaves can be stored for a long time without losing their resilience. Keep them in the salad compartment of the fridge and they will stay fresh for up to

Left: Chinese leaves have a crunchy texture and a delicate aroma. The mild cabbage flavour disappears when the vegetable is cooked.

10–12 days. Don't worry if there are tiny black specks on the leaves as this is quite normal and will not do any harm.

Preparing Chinese leaves

1 Discard any damaged outer leaves and trim off the root.

2 It is not usually necessary to wash the leaves, simply cut the head of Chinese leaves crossways into thin shreds.

3 You may prefer to wash the leaves, before using in a salad, for instance. Separate the leaves, then wash under cold running water. Shake off any excess water before shredding.

Right: Dark green bok choy tastes similar to spinach. The white stems can be cooked and eaten separately.

BOK CHOY/PAK-CHOI

MANDARIN: *XIAO BAICAI;*
CANTONESE: *BOK CHOI*

Another member of the brassica family, bok choy goes by lots of different names. In the West it is sometimes known as *pak-choi,* horse's ear (from the shape of the leaves) or Chinese white cabbage. In Cantonese, the name means simply white vegetable, which is a bit of a misnomer, as the glossy leaves that are a distinctive feature of this vegetable are dark green. The stalks, however, are pale, and range from light green to ivory white. Bok choy is a perennial, and several varieties are available throughout the year.

Aroma and flavour

Although bok choy is less delicate and does not taste as sweet as Chinese leaves, it has a distinctive flavour, which is a sort of cross between a mild cabbage and spinach.

Culinary uses

Bok choy and Chinese leaves are interchangeable in most dishes, even though their colour and flavour are different. Bok choy can be used in soups and stir-fries, and is delicious when quickly braised, but should not be subjected to prolonged stewing.

Preparation and cooking techniques

Bok choy is prepared in much the same way as Chinese leaves, except that the stems are as important (some would say more important) than the leaves. It is a good idea to separate leaves and stems for cooking, as the latter take slightly longer. Baby bok choy can be cooked whole or in halves or quarters. Only when very young and tender can bok choy be eaten raw.

Storage

Bok choy is completely different from Chinese leaves when it comes to storage. Try to use it as soon as you buy it, because the leaves will start to wilt, and the outer leaves will turn yellow, after 2–3 days, much sooner than lettuce and spinach.

Below: Bright green choi sum is easy to prepare.

CHOI SUM

MANDARIN: *YOU CAIXIN;*
CANTONESE: *CHOI SUM*

Choi sum is a Cantonese word, meaning "cabbage heart". A member of the brassica family, it is related to oilseed rape. It has bright green leaves and thin, pale green stalks that are slightly grooved. The bright yellow flowers at the centre are responsible for its common name of Chinese flowering cabbage.

Aroma and flavour

Choi sum has a pleasant aroma with a mild taste, and remains crisp and tender if correctly cooked.

Culinary uses

A very popular green vegetable, choi sum can be used for soups or stir-fries, either solo or with other ingredients.

Preparation and cooking techniques

Little preparation is required, just wash and shake off excess water before cutting the leaves to the required size. Most restaurant chefs leave the stalks whole, simply blanching them in stock for a minute or two before draining them and serving with oyster sauce.

Preparing choi sum

Choi sum is easy to prepare. You can chop leaves and stalks into large pieces before cooking, but they are more often left whole.

Wash choi sum under cold running water, then shake off the excess water and separate the stalks before use.

Storage

Choi sum can be kept in the salad compartment of a fridge for 3–4 days if bought fresh, but should ideally be used as quickly as possible.

MUSTARD GREENS

MANDARIN: *GAICAI*; CANTONESE: *GAI CHOI*

Although this vegetable is related to choi sum it looks and tastes completely different. In shape, it resembles a Cos lettuce. Unlike many oriental vegetables, which were relatively unknown outside their country of origin until recently, mustard greens have long been cultivated in Europe. However, the dark green, slightly puckered leaves were always thrown away; only the seeds were prized. It took the Chinese to introduce us to their delicious flavour. Mustard greens are most abundant during the winter and spring, especially from Asian groceries, but also from specialist producers and farm shops.

Aroma and flavour

Although mustard greens look a bit like lettuces, there the resemblance ends. The leaves have a robust, often fiery flavour. They can taste quite bitter.

Culinary uses

Very young leaves can be eaten raw in salads; mature leaves are best stir-fried or simmered in soups. In China, most of the crop is salted and preserved.

Preparation and cooking techniques

Before being stir-fried, mustard greens benefit from being blanched in lightly salted boiling water or stock; this preserves the green colour of the leaves and also gets rid of some of the bitter taste.

Storage

Provided that they are fresh when you buy them, mustard greens will keep for a few days if stored in the salad compartment of a fridge.

CHINESE BROCCOLI

CHINESE: *GAILAN*

Chinese broccoli has more in common with purple sprouting broccoli than the plump, tight heads of Calabrese broccoli familiar to Western shoppers. The Chinese version has long, slender stems, loose leaves and can be recognized by the tiny white or yellow flowers in the centre.

Aroma and flavour

As its Chinese name *gailan* (mustard orchid) implies, Chinese broccoli belongs to the same family as mustard greens, but is more robust, both in terms of texture and of taste. There is a definite cabbage flavour.

Culinary uses

Every part of this beautiful vegetable is edible – the flower, leaves and stalk – and each has its own individual flavour and texture. Chinese broccoli is often served on its own as a side dish, but it can also be combined with other ingredients that have contrasting colours, flavours and textures.

Preparation and cooking techniques

Discard the tough outer leaves, then peel off any tough skin from the stalks. Leave each stalk whole if it is to be served on its own, or cut into two to three short sections if it is to be cooked with other ingredients. Before stir-frying it is usual to blanch the vegetable briefly in salted boiling water or in stock, which will enhance the flavour.

Storage

Chinese broccoli will keep for only 2–3 days even if it is very fresh when bought; after that the leaves will start to wilt and go yellow, and the stalks are liable to become tough.

Right: Every part of Chinese broccoli is edible.

AUBERGINE

MANDARIN: *QIEZI*; CANTONESE: *NGAI GWA*

There are numerous varieties of this wonderfully versatile vegetable, which is technically a fruit. Although it belongs to the same family as peppers and tomatoes, which originated in America, the aubergine is actually native to tropical Asia, where it has been cultivated for more than 2,000 years.

The most common type in Asia – the Asian or Japanese aubergine – is tubular rather than ovoid in shape and is usually straight or slightly curved. As a rule, Asian aubergines tend to be much smaller and more slender than western varieties, and some are tiny. In Thailand, there are aubergines that are not much bigger than peas. Aubergines come in a wide range of colours, from black through purple, orange and green to the white egg-shaped vegetables that inspired the vegetable's American name of eggplant.

Right: Thai baby aubergines

Below: Purple and green aubergines from Thailand

Aroma and flavour

Whatever its shape, size or colour, the aubergine has a unique flavour that is almost impossible to describe. Some object to its smoky, subtly bitter taste, others prize it for the same reason.

Culinary uses

Aubergine absorbs the flavours of other ingredients like a sponge, and therefore benefits from being cooked with strongly flavoured foods and seasonings. It can be stir-fried, deep-fried, stuffed and baked, braised, steamed, or served cold, but seldom eaten raw except in Thailand, where strips of very young aubergine are served like crudités, with spicy dips.

Preparation and cooking techniques

Wash and remove the stalk, then cut into slices, strips or chunks. It is seldom necessary to peel an aubergine, and the smooth skin not only adds a beautiful colour, but also provides the dish with an interesting texture and flavour.

Some recipes advise layering aubergine slices with salt before cooking. This is not essential if the vegetables are young and tender, but in older specimens this is done to reduce bitterness and to prevent the slices from absorbing excessive amounts of oil during cooking. If you do salt an aubergine, be sure to rinse and dry it thoroughly afterwards.

Another method that stops the aubergine from drawing up too much oil, but which has the advantage of retaining the succulent texture, is to dry-fry the strips or slices over a medium heat for 4–5 minutes before cooking them in hot oil.

Storage

Aubergines from various parts of the world are available all year round. Select small- to medium-size firm aubergines with a uniformly smooth skin that is free from blemishes. Large specimens with a shrivelled skin are overmature and are likely to be bitter and rather tough.

When bought in prime condition, aubergines will keep for 3–4 days in the salad compartment of the fridge.

CHAYOTE

CANTONESE: *FAT SAU GWA*

There are several names for this pear-shaped marrow, vegetable pear being one, and custard marrow being another. In the Caribbean they know it as christophine, but in other parts of the world it is *choko, shu-shu* or *chinchayote*. The Chinese call it "Buddha's fist", because it resembles hands clasped in prayer, with the fingers folded inside.

Aroma and flavour

Chayote has a smooth, pale green skin with a subtle aroma. The taste is delicate, and the texture is fairly firm, not unlike that of courgette.

Culinary uses

Because of the religious connotations of its shape, chayote is often used as an offering during Buddhist festivals. It can be eaten raw or cooked, and in Asia is usually stir-fried or simmered in soups.

Preparation and cooking techniques

Wash but do not peel the vegetable, cut it open and remove the stone from the centre, then cut into thin slices or strips. Since chayote has a mild taste, Asian cooks often cook it with strong seasonings such as garlic, ginger, onion and/or chillies.

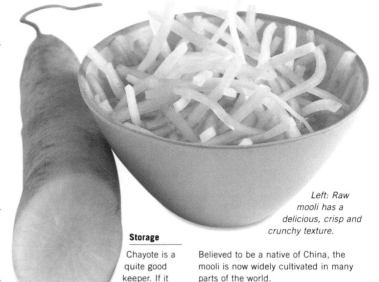

Left: Raw mooli has a delicious, crisp and crunchy texture.

Storage

Chayote is a quite good keeper. If it is hard and smooth, it will stay fresh for up to a week if stored in the salad compartment of the fridge.

MOOLI/DAIKON

MANDARIN: *LUOBO*; CANTONESE: *LOH BAK*; VIETNAMESE: *LOBAC*; MALAY: *LAPHUG*

This large, thin cylindrical vegetable looks rather like a carrot, but with a smooth, white skin. A member of the radish family, it is sometimes known as the oriental radish.

Above: Chayote can be eaten raw, stir-fried or cooked in soups.

Believed to be a native of China, the mooli is now widely cultivated in many parts of the world.

Aroma and flavour

Mooli has an unmistakable, pungent smell of radish. The texture is crisp and crunchy and it tastes quite mild, with a juicy, sweet flavour similar to turnip.

Culinary uses

Mooli can be eaten raw or cooked. Both the Chinese and the Japanese also pickle it. Cantonese cooks use it to make a stiff pudding with rice flour, which is often served as part of the dim sum selection in a restaurant. At home, mooli is usually braised with meat such as pork or beef, but it is also delicious in a stir-fry. Add it for the last few minutes of cooking so that the slices stay crisp and juicy.

Preparation and cooking techniques

Like carrots, mooli should be scraped or peeled, then cut into slices or chunks before cooking. The beauty of this vegetable is that it withstands long cooking without disintegrating, and absorbs the flavours of other ingredients, but also tastes good raw.

Storage

Buy mooli with firm, unblemished skin. Stored in a cool, dark place or in the salad compartment of the fridge, it should keep for 3–4 days.

BITTER MELON

MANDARIN: *KUGUA;* CANTONESE: *FOO GWA*

Also called "bitter gourd", this warty-skinned vegetable originated in South-east Asia, and is popular in Indonesia, the Philippines and Thailand, where it is used as the basis for a delicious curry. The plant resembles a wild grape vine, and is grown in the West mainly as an ornament, for its attractive foliage and strange-looking fruit.

Aroma and flavour

As the name implies, the flesh of this vegetable tastes quite bitter, especially when it is green and immature, but it has a rather sweet and fragrant smell. The flavour mellows somewhat as the vegetable ripens and turns first pale green and then yellow-orange (when it is past its prime).

Culinary uses

Bitterness may be an acquired taste, but it has a cooling effect in a hot climate, and is highly regarded in Asia. The flesh readily absorbs other flavours and its bitter tang can provide a wonderful accent in a dish.

Preparation and cooking

Since the odd-looking skin is a special feature of this vegetable, it is never peeled. Just wash it, slice it in half lengthways, remove and discard the seeds, then cut into slices or chunks. Blanch these in lightly salted boiling water for about 2 minutes to remove excess bitterness, then drain before stir-frying or adding to soups.

Right: In China and Thailand winter melon is made into a soup and served in the shell.

Storage

Firm, green bitter melon will keep for 3–4 days (and should be allowed to ripen a little before use), but a soft yellowish one should be used within a day or two.

WINTER MELON

CHINESE: *DONG GUA*

This is one of the largest vegetables grown in Asia, or anywhere else. They can grow to 25cm/10in in diameter, and weigh more than 25kg/55lb. Thankfully for the cook, there are small ones, and the larger melons are normally sliced and sold in sections.

Above: Despite its name, bitter melon has a sweet smell.

Aroma and flavour

Winter melon has a subtle, delicate smell. It tastes rather like courgette.

Culinary uses

Despite its name, winter melon is really a warm season vegetable, and since more than 90 per cent of it is water, it is popular in hot weather as it is juicy yet not too filling. It is always cooked before being eaten.

Preparation and cooking

Winter melon is prepared in much the same way as pumpkin. The rind must be cut off and the seeds and coarse fibres at the centre scooped out before the flesh is cut into thin strips or wedges. It tastes good in stir-fries or soups. Winter melon readily absorbs other flavours, and is often cooked with strongly-flavoured ingredients such as dried shrimps, ham and dried mushrooms.

Storage

A whole winter melon will keep for days if not weeks, but if it has been sliced open, it should be eaten as soon as possible as the exposed surface will deteriorate rapidly.

ONIONS

MANDARIN: *YANG CONG;* CANTONESE: *YUN TS'UNG*

The common onion so widely used in the West is known as "foreign onion" in Asia, where shallots and spring onions are generally preferred. They come in a wide variety of sizes and colours from huge golden-skinned globes to smaller, milder red and white onions.

Aroma and flavour

There is no mistaking the strong aroma and flavour of the onion. It is used as a flavouring ingredient throughout Asia, but is seldom served on its own as a side vegetable.

Culinary uses

The onion is a very versatile vegetable. It can be eaten fried, boiled, steamed or raw, and it is an essential component of a great number of sauces and dishes, such as curries and stews. Fried onions are a popular garnish, especially in South-east Asia.

Above: Small and large onions

Preparation and cooking techniques

Peel the onions and remove the papery skin, then slice and chop as required. A good tip for avoiding irritation to the eyes when cutting an onion is to leave the root in place until the last minute, and, when the root is exposed, to press it down on the surface of the chopping board rather than expose it to the air.

Storage

If you buy firm onions with smooth, unmarked skins, and store them in a cool, dry place, they will keep for several weeks. If any show signs of sprouting, use them immediately.

SHALLOTS

MANDARIN: *FEN CONG;* CANTONESE: *TS'UNG TAU;* THAI: *HOM DAENG*

Although they belong to the same family as garlic, leeks, chives and onions – and look suspiciously like baby onions – shallots are very much their own vegetable. Sometimes called bunching onions, they have bulbs that multiply to produce clusters joined at the root end.

Aroma and flavour

Shallots tend to be sweeter and much milder than large onions. Some Thai varieties are sweet enough to be used in desserts.

Above: Small red onions

Culinary uses

Indispensable in South-east Asian kitchens, shallots are far more popular than both regular onions and spring onions for everyday use. Minced with garlic, ginger and other aromatics, shallots form the standard marinade and are also an essential ingredient in curry pastes and satay sauce. Dried shallots *(hanh huong)* are a popular alternative in Vietnam.

Preparation and cooking techniques

Top and tail the shallots, peel off the skin, then prize the bulbs apart. Leave these whole for braising, or chop as required. Thinly-sliced shallot rings are sometimes dry-fried until crisp, then used as a garnish.

Storage

Shallots will keep for several months in a cool, dry place.

SPRING ONIONS

MANDARIN: *QING CONG;* CANTONESE: *TS'UNG;* JAPANESE: *NEGI*

Spring onions, known as green onions or scallions in the West, have been cultivated in China and Japan since time immemorial. The leaves are tubular, and are always sold with the small white onion bulb attached. Japanese spring onions are larger than the European variety and have blue-green stems.

Aroma and flavour

Spring onions have a more subtle smell than onions and the taste can vary from fairly mild to really pungent. Smaller bulbs generally have a milder flavour.

Left: Spring onions

How to make spring onion curls

1 Trim off most of the green leaves from the spring onion bulbs to leave a 7.5cm/3in length.

2 Finely shred the spring onions to within about 1cm/½in of the root end.

3 Place the shredded spring onions in a bowl of iced water and chill for 15–20 minutes or until the shredded ends have curled.

Culinary uses

In Asia, spring onions are served as a vegetable as well as being used as a flavouring agent. The vegetable forms a yin-yang pair when used in combination with ginger. Spring onions are yin, and ginger is yang.

Preparation and cooking techniques

Trim off the roots from the bulbs and discard any wilted outer leaves, then separate the green and white parts, and cut these into short lengths or shreds. Recipes sometimes stipulate that only the white parts are used. If spring onion green is used in a recipe, it is usually added at the last moment (the white part takes longer to cook) or is simply used raw, as a garnish.

Storage

It is best not to keep spring onions in a plastic bag, but instead to store them loose in the salad drawer of the fridge in order to allow them to "breathe". That way they should stay fresh for up to 4–5 days if bought in prime condition.

CHINESE CHIVES

MANDARIN: *JIUCAI*; CANTONESE: *GAU CHOI*

Although they belong to the same family, Chinese chives are quite different from the Western variety, both in their appearance and taste. Two species are available: one has long, flat green leaves like a small, thin leek, the other has long, tubular stalks with a single bud at the tip.

Aroma and flavour

Chinese chives have a much stronger aroma

Right: Chinese chives

than the ones grown in the West. They don't really taste of onions, but have a flavour that resembles a cross between garlic and leek.

Culinary uses

Chinese chives are seldom used as a garnish, but are either served as a vegetable in their own right, or used as an ingredient in cooked dishes, especially with seafood or meat. A very popular Chinese vegetarian dish features chopped chives cooked with scrambled eggs and beancurd. This is not only colourful, but tastes delicious.

Preparation and cooking techniques

Chinese chives are always sold as leaves only, without the bulb. Uniformly dark green leaves are good, and any that are turning yellow should be discarded. Wash well, drain, then chop or slice into short sections. Cantonese cooks often blanch chives in boiling water or stock for a minute or two before stir-frying.

Storage

Fresh chives stored in an airtight box in the fridge should keep for 4–5 days.

POTATOES AND SWEET POTATOES

MANDARIN: *PENSHU;* CANTONESE: *FAN SHUE*

Although potatoes and sweet potatoes are unrelated, this was not appreciated when they first reached Asia, and they were both given the same Chinese name. In northern China white potatoes are a staple food, although not as important as noodles; in southern China they are far less significant. Sweet potatoes are popular in the Philippines.

Aroma and flavour

Several varieties of both regular potatoes and sweet potatoes are grown in the East, so tubers vary in size, shape and colour, as well as in taste and texture. The sweet potatoes have a red skin and flesh that varies from pale white to yellow-orange in colour.

Culinary uses

Where potatoes are used, they generally form part of a braised dish, or are served as a side dish or snack. Potato flour is a popular thickener.

Preparation and cooking techniques

Both regular potatoes and sweet potatoes are prepared in the same way: after peeling, they are sliced or diced, then stir-fried or braised with seasonings or spices. Thai cooks make a very sweet dessert based on deep-fried sweet potatoes.

Above: Potatoes and sweet potatoes

Storage

Potatoes should always be stored in a cool, dark, dry place. Because of their high sugar content, sweet potatoes do not keep well.

TAROES

MANDARIN: *YUTOU;* CANTONESE: *WOO TAU*

These tubers grow in tropical areas and are widely used throughout South-east Asia. There are two basic varieties: the big, barrel-shaped one with the hairy brown skin is the most common, but there is also a smaller variety which is known in the West as eddo or dasheen. The flesh is white, with purple flecks.

Aroma and flavour

Cooked taro has a subtle flavour that has been described as resembling floury water chestnuts.

Culinary uses

Taroes can be substituted for potatoes in most dishes. They take up a great deal of liquid, so are good in stews. Asian cooks often include taro when cooking belly pork or duck as it absorbs the excess fat.

Above: A barrel-shaped taro

Preparation and cooking techniques

It is essential to cook taroes as there are toxins just below the skin. These are eliminated when the vegetable is boiled. Peel the vegetables thickly, wearing gloves, or cook them in their jackets.

Storage

Store in a cool, dark, dry place. Taroes have a thick skin, so they keep well.

YAMS

MANDARIN: *SHANYAO;* CANTONESE: *SA GOT*

Yams are believed to have originated in China, but are now grown in all tropical regions. The Chinese yam has fine whiskers and the flesh is creamy white.

Aroma and flavour

Yams do not have a pronounced flavour, but are mildly sweet and quite juicy.

Culinary uses

Like taroes, yams can be used instead of potatoes. Asian cooks often use them as a substitute for bamboo shoots.

Preparation and cooking techniques

Peel yams thickly, removing both the outer skin and the layer underneath. Like taroes, they contain a toxin that is eliminated when boiled. Slice or dice the flesh and put into salted water.

Storage

As for taroes.

LOTUS ROOT

MANDARIN: *LIAN OU;* CANTONESE: *LEEN NGAU*

Lotus root, also known as *renkon*, is used throughout Asia and is particularly popular in China and Japan. Raw lotus root looks like a string of fat sausages covered in black mud. Clean, peel and slice it, however, and a beautiful pattern emerges in each cross-section, the result of narrow channels that run through the root. Fresh lotus roots can sometimes be purchased from Asian stores. Canned lotus root is readily available, and dried slices are popular for serving in soups.

Aroma and flavour

The root has very little aroma, but the flavour is mild and subtly sweet. It has a wonderful crunchy texture.

Culinary uses

Apart from the root being used as a vegetable, the seeds of the lotus are eaten as a delicate fruit when fresh, or used as a dessert in dried form. They can also be puréed and blended with sugar to make a filling for cakes and buns. Dried lotus leaves are used for wrapping food in a number of famous Asian dishes.

Preparation and cooking techniques

Fresh lotus roots must be scrubbed. Chop them into sections, discarding the tough "necks" between, then peel off the outer skin. The sliced flesh is usually

Above: Lotus root and seeds

sliced or cut into large chunks, but whole roots can also be stuffed. Japanese cooks often soak the slices in water acidulated with rice vinegar for 5 minutes before boiling them. They cook quickly and make a pretty garnish. Dried lotus roots are sold sliced, and should be soaked in water for 1–2 hours before using in soups or stews. Canned lotus roots are ready for use.

Storage

Fresh lotus root should keep for about 4 days if bought in good condition. Select firm and unblemished roots. If the surface is punctured, dirt will have penetrated inside, which makes the roots difficult to clean. Dried roots will keep almost indefinitely if stored in a dry, cool place.

DRIED LILY BUDS

MANDARIN: *HUANG HUA; JINZHEN*
CANTONESE: *GUM JUM*

Also known in Chinese as "yellow flower" or "golden needles", these dried buds of the tiger lily are popular throughout China and South-east Asia.

Aroma and flavour

Tiger lily has a unique fragrance, which intensifies when the buds are dried. They have a mild sweet taste and a pleasant crunchy texture.

Culinary uses

In Chinese cooking, dried lily buds are often combined with dried black fungus to create an interesting contrast in colour, flavour and texture. The buds are also a popular ingredient in Buddhist vegetarian cooking.

Preparation and cooking techniques

Dried lily buds must be soaked in warm water for 30 minutes or so, then drained and rinsed in cold water until clean. Once the hard ends have been snipped off, the buds can be used whole, or cut in half.

Storage

Dried lily buds keep almost indefinitely if stored in an airtight jar, away from strong light, heat or moisture.

Below: Lily buds are never used fresh, but always dried.

the canned ones, but need more preparation. They must be soaked in water for 2–3 hours before use.

Storage

Fresh shoots will keep for up to a week in winter, but only 2–3 days in summer. Unused shoots from a can will keep in the fridge for several days if stored in a jar of fresh water that is changed daily. Dried shoots will keep almost indefinitely in a cool, dry place.

BEANSPROUTS

MANDARIN: *DOUYA;*
CANTONESE: *DAU NGA CHOI*

Several types of bean can be sprouted, but the ones most often used in Asian cooking are the small "green" sprouts from mung beans and the larger "yellow" or soya bean sprouts. The fresh sprouts are widely available in supermarkets, health food shops and markets, or you can sprout the beans at home. Avoid canned beansprouts, which are limp and tasteless.

BAMBOO SHOOTS

MANDARIN: *ZHUSUN;* CANTONESE: *CHUK SUN;*
JAPANESE: *TAKENOKO*

Bamboo is one of the most important plants of eastern Asia, and several species are grown, of varying sizes. The shoots used as a vegetable are dug just before they come above ground. Fresh bamboo shoots are difficult to come by outside Asia, but canned shoots are readily available. Vietnamese cooks are fond of pickled bamboo shoots.

Aroma and flavour

The aroma of bamboo shoots is quite delicate. Lovers of this vegetable – and they are legion – claim that the mild sweet flavour changes subtly with the seasons. Therefore winter bamboo shoots are more highly prized.

Culinary uses

In China, where bamboo shoots have been eaten for well over a thousand years, they are regarded as the queen of all vegetables. The shoots not only taste delicious of themselves, but also complement the flavours of other ingredients with which they are cooked.

Above: Chunks of raw bamboo shoot and canned slices

Preparation and cooking techniques

If you are lucky enough to locate fresh bamboo shoots, it is vital to parboil them before cooking, as they contain an acid that is highly toxic. Remove the base and the hard outer leaves, then cut the core into large chunks. Boil these in salted water for 20–30 minutes, then drain, rinse in clean water and drain again. Cut into slices, shreds or cubes for further cooking. Canned bamboo shoots are ready cooked, so they just need to be rinsed and drained before using them. Dried bamboo shoots have been dried in the sun, so they are tastier than

Right: Mung bean sprouts (in bowl) and soya bean sprouts

Aroma and flavour

Soya bean sprouts have a stronger flavour than mung bean sprouts, but both are relatively delicate, with a pleasant crunchy texture.

Culinary uses

Stir-frying, with or without meat, is the most popular way of cooking beansprouts. Mung bean sprouts can be eaten raw in salads, while soya bean sprouts are often used in soups.

Preparation and cooking techniques

Wash the beansprouts in cold water to remove the husks and tiny roots. Some restaurants actually top and tail each individual shoot, which turns this humble vegetable into a luxury dish. Since the sprouts are largely composed of water, overcooking will render them limp and fibrous, and the characteristic crisp texture will be lost.

Storage

In order to preserve their lily-white translucence, keep beansprouts in water in a covered box in the fridge. They will stay fresh for 2–3 days.

WATER CHESTNUTS

MANDARIN: *BIQI;* CANTONESE: *MA TAI*

Water chestnuts are popular throughout Asia, cropping up in Chinese, Japanese, Korean and South-east Asian recipes. The name is slightly misleading as they do grow in water (and are actually cultivated in paddy fields) but they certainly aren't nuts. Instead, they are corms, which are about the size of walnuts. There are several varieties, but the Chinese type, which are dark brown and look a bit like small daffodil bulbs, are the most widely available outside Asia. They have a soft skin which, because they grow in water, tends to be covered in dried dirt. Fresh water chestnuts are superior to canned.

Aroma and flavour

The best thing about water chestnuts is their texture. The snow-white flesh is crunchy and juicy, and stays that way,

no matter how long they are cooked for. This, coupled with their pleasantly sweet taste, makes them irresistible.

Culinary uses

Water chestnuts can be eaten raw in both savoury and fruit salads. In many Asian countries they are eaten as a snack food, in much the same way as peanuts are eaten in the West. Cooked water chestnuts taste wonderful in stir-fries or braised dishes. The flesh is also made into a flour, which is used both as a thickening agent and in cakes.

Preparation and cooking techniques

Fresh water chestnuts are not very appealing, especially as they are usually covered in dried mud, but once they are washed and peeled, they do not look very different from the canned variety. Water chestnuts can be left whole, sliced or diced, and are sometimes minced with fish or meat.

Storage

Fresh, unpeeled water chestnuts will keep well if stored in a paper bag in the vegetable crisper in the fridge. Once peeled, however, fresh water chestnuts must be kept in water in a covered container in the fridge and should be used within a week.

Horned water chestnuts
This nut is often confused with the vegetable of the same name, but they look entirely different. Horned water chestnuts (*ling gok*), which have been eaten in China for hundreds of years, have a hard, shiny black shell with two distinctive, sharp horns. The nuts measure about 5cm/2in from tip to tip, and the shells, which are extremely difficult to crack, enclose ivory coloured flesh that is starchy and sweet tasting. The nuts are never eaten raw, but can be steamed or boiled and served like a vegetable, added to soups or braised in stews.
 Horned water chestnuts can be bought in Asian and Chinese shops and will keep fresh for several weeks in the fridge. However, once shelled the flesh, which should be white and unblemished, needs to be used within a day or two as it quickly becomes rancid.

Below: Canned water chestnuts (in bowl) and fresh water chestnut corms, which look a little like small daffodil bulbs.

MANGETOUTS

MANDARIN: *XUEDOU;* CANTONESE: *HOH LAN DAU*

Also known as snow peas, mangetouts must be one of the best known and best loved of all oriental vegetables, yet its Cantonese name, meaning Dutch bean, suggests that at some point in its long history it was perceived as being of Western origin. The French name – *mangetout* – means "eat all" and is an apt description, for the vegetable is valued for its pods, not the peas, which never mature. Sugar snap peas are similar, but have slightly plumper pods.

Aroma and flavour

Freshly picked mangetouts have a fresh aroma, but this vanishes quite quickly. The flavour is slightly sweet. The best way to appreciate these delicate, tender pods is to stir-fry them, when they will prove perfect partners for prawns, scallops and other shellfish.

Preparation and cooking techniques

Mangetouts need very little by way of preparation. Simply wash, then top and tail the pods. It should not be necessary to string them if the pods are young and tender. Leave whole if small; snap in half if large. Stir-fry on their own, or with other vegetables such as carrots, spring onions and baby corn cobs, in hot oil over high heat for a short time, and do not use too much seasoning.

Storage

Young, crisp and unblemished mangetouts with thin skins will keep fresh for up to 4–5 days in the salad compartment of the fridge.

SNAKE BEANS/GREEN BEANS

MANDARIN: *DOUJIAO* CANTONESE: *DAU GOK*

Also called yard-long beans, asparagus beans or Thai beans, these resemble French beans but are much longer. There are two

Above: Snake beans are also known as yard-long beans.

varieties: a pale green type, and a darker green one that is considered to be better. Thinner beans are best.

Aroma and flavour

These exceptionally long beans smell and taste rather like their French cousins, but the flavour is not identical. When young they are slightly sweeter and more tender, but the mature beans can be tough, and may need slightly longer cooking than French beans.

Culinary uses

Snake beans are usually stir-fried, either on their own or with other ingredients, or served cold as a salad after blanching. They are also delicious blanched and tossed in sesame oil.

Preparation and cooking techniques

Having washed the beans, cut them into 5cm/2in lengths. They go particularly well with shredded pork, chicken or prawns, and should only be lightly seasoned. In Sichuan, they are used for a dish called *kan shao* (dry-frying), with strongly flavoured seasonings such as garlic, ginger or chillies.

Storage

Try to use snake beans within about 3 days of purchase before they turn yellow and become stringy.

Right: Mangetouts (top) and sugar snap peas

LUFFA

MANDARIN: *SIGUA;*
CANTONESE: *SZE GWA*

Also known as angled luffa, silk gourd, silk squash or Chinese okra, this vegetable looks like a long, skinny courgette or a very large okra pod. The most common variety is ridged down its length and is dark green in colour. Although not so common, smooth luffa is larger and the shape is more cylindrical, with a slightly thicker base. It is much heavier than ridged luffa, and is lighter in colour.

Aroma and flavour

Luffa has a mild, delicate taste, very similar to that of cucumber and the two are interchangeable in most cooked dishes.

Culinary uses

Used mostly in stir-fries and soups, luffa goes well with foods that will not overwhelm its delicate flavour, such as chicken breast, fish and seafood. It is also a popular ingredient in all kinds of vegetable dishes.

Preparation and cooking techniques

If the luffa is young, all you need to do is wash and slice it. Luffas seldom need peeling, but sometimes the ridges toughen as the vegetable ripens, in

Above: A whole luffa and slices

which case remove the ridges but leave the skin between, so that the luffa is striped green and white. If the skin is very tough, it is best to peel it completely. Like cucumber, luffa should not be overcooked, but unlike cucumber, it is never eaten raw.

Above: Crunchy-textured baby corn cobs make a colourful addition to stir-fries.

Storage

Keep fresh luffa in the vegetable compartment of the fridge, but do not store it for too long as within two or three days of purchase it will start to go limp.

BABY CORN COBS

MANDARIN: *YUMI SUN;*
CANTONESE: *YOOK MY SON*

Baby corn cobs are available both fresh and canned. The canned ones can be quite large, and are not as tender and delicate as the smaller, fresh cobs.

Aroma and flavour

Baby corn has a lovely sweet fragrance and flavour, as well as an irresistible crunchy texture.

Culinary uses

The baby cobs can be used in salads, stir-fries and soups. In stir-fries, they add colour as well as flavour, and are good combined with carrots, peppers, broccoli and mangetouts.

Preparation and cooking techniques

Wash the cobs. Large ones can be halved lengthways or sliced in thick diagonal chunks, but small ones are best left whole. Asian cooks blanch them in lightly salted water for 1 minute before stir-frying. Drain and rinse canned cobs before use. Do not overcook them.

Storage

Fresh baby corn cobs will keep for up to a week in the salad compartment of the fridge, but they are best eaten soon after purchase.

FRESH AND DRIED MUSHROOMS

SHIITAKE

MANDARIN: *XIANG GU*; CANTONESE: *HUNG GWO*; JAPANESE: *SHIITAKE*

Fresh shiitake mushrooms used to be a rarity in the West, but are now cultivated and are freely available in supermarkets. They resemble large, brown button mushrooms in appearance, but are actually a type of fungus that grows on hardwood logs in their native Japan. Shiitake mushrooms are frequently dried (see Dried Black Mushrooms, overleaf) and are also available in cans.

Aroma and flavour

These meaty mushrooms taste slightly acidic, and have a decidedly slippery texture. They contain twice as much protein as button mushrooms. When shiitake are dried the flavour intensifies.

Culinary uses

Although small mushrooms can be eaten raw, cooking brings out their flavour. They are used in soups, stir-fries and braised dishes. They are a popular ingredient in vegetarian dishes, and go well with noodles and rice. They are good combined with less strongly flavoured food.

Below: Fresh and dried shiitake mushrooms

Preparation and cooking techniques

The stems of fresh shiitake mushrooms are usually removed before cooking. Whole or sliced caps can be sautéed, used in stir-fries, cooked in braised dishes or added to soups. Because of their robust texture, shiitake need a slightly longer cooking time than button mushrooms, but they should not be cooked for too long or they may begin to toughen. To serve shiitake mushrooms in a salad, boil

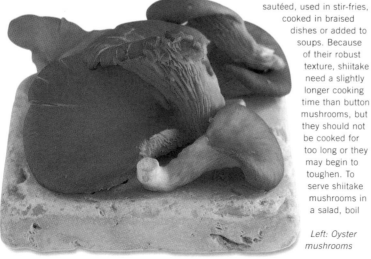

Left: Oyster mushrooms

them briefly in water or stock, then cool them slightly and toss in a French dressing before serving.

Storage

Store fresh shiitake mushrooms in a paper bag in the fridge. Eat within three days of purchase.

OYSTER MUSHROOMS

MANDARIN: *BAOYU GU*; CANTONESE: *HOWYOO GWO*; JAPANESE: *SHIMEJI*

In the wild, oyster mushrooms grow in clumps on rotting wood.The caps, gills and stems are all the same colour, which can be pearl grey, pink or yellow. Once thought of exclusively as wild mushrooms, they are now grown commercially and are widely available in Western supermarkets.

Aroma and flavour

The flavour is fairly mild, with a slight suggestion of seafood.

Culinary uses

Oyster mushrooms are popular in soups and stir-fries, and they are also used in noodle and rice dishes.

Preparation and cooking techniques

Oyster mushrooms seldom need trimming. Large ones should be torn, rather than cut into pieces. The soft texture becomes rubbery if they are overcooked, so always add them to cooked dishes at the last moment.

Storage

Buy oyster mushrooms that smell and look fresh, avoiding any with damp, slimy patches and those that have discoloured. Store in a paper bag in vegetable compartment of the fridge, and use as soon as possible after purchase. They do not keep for more than 2–3 days.

ENOKI MUSHROOMS

MANDARIN: *JINZHEN GU;* CANTONESE: *GUM JUM GWO;* JAPANESE: *ENO ITAKE*

Also called *enokitaki,* these are slender and exceedingly delicate mushrooms with long thin stems and tiny white caps. The Chinese name – "golden needle mushrooms" – is the same as that given to the dried tiger lily buds which they resemble. Fresh enoki mushrooms are popular in both China and Japan. Avoid canned ones.

Aroma and flavour

Enoki mushrooms have a delicate sweet and almost fruity flavour, and a deliciously crisp texture.

Above: Enoki mushrooms have pretty, tiny caps on elegant long stalks.

Culinary uses

The delicate flavour of enoki mushrooms is best appreciated if they are added raw to salads or lightly cooked and used as a garnish for soups or hot dishes.

Preparation and cooking techniques

The mushrooms are harvested in clumps, attached to a spongy root base which is cut off before use. The

mushrooms are then ready for use. They rapidly toughen if overcooked, so are usually added to soups or braised dishes shortly before serving. They are good in stir-fried dishes, too, but should not be cooked for longer than 1 minute.

Storage

If bought fresh, enoki mushrooms will keep for 4–5 days in the salad compartment of a fridge. Avoid any that have damp, slimy patches and those that have discoloured.

STRAW MUSHROOMS

MANDARIN: *CAOGU;* CANTONESE: *TSO GWO*

These small, grey-brown mushrooms are grown on beds of rice straw, hence the name. A native of China, they were introduced to South-east Asia by Chinese immigrants.

Aroma and flavour

Fresh straw mushrooms are not readily available in the West, but dried ones can sometimes be found in Asian or Chinese stores. Straw mushrooms have an even stronger aroma than Chinese dried black mushrooms. Canned straw mushrooms are widely available in Asian stores; they have a delicate, silky surface with a subtle, sweet taste and an unusual slippery texture.

Culinary uses

Because they have an almost neutral flavour, straw mushrooms can be combined with all sorts of ingredients in stir-fries, braised dishes and soups. They are an essential ingredient in many Chinese dishes, and they are also used for making mushroom soy sauce.

Preparation and cooking techniques

Canned straw mushrooms must be drained and thoroughly rinsed before use. They are usually cut in half lengthways. This not only reveals the rather attractive "umbrella" pattern, but

Below: Sliced straw mushrooms, showing their attractive "umbrella" pattern.

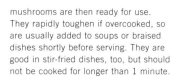

it also makes them much easier to pick up with chopsticks. Like all mushrooms, straw mushrooms must not be overcooked, especially the canned ones, as they have been cooked already.

Storage

Fresh straw mushrooms are difficult to store, which explains why they are not often seen outside Asia. Dried ones can be stored almost indefinitely, though they may lose some of their flavour.

DRIED BLACK MUSHROOMS/ FRAGRANT MUSHROOMS

Dried black mushrooms are widely used throughout Asia, and are exported around the world. Although they are frequently labelled as "Chinese", to distinguish them from other dried mushrooms, and have come to be widely known as such, the majority of dried black mushrooms sold in Asian stores actually come from Japan, which produces and exports far more dried black mushrooms than does China.

Aroma and flavour

There are generally three different grades of dried black mushrooms, with caps that range in colour from dark grey, to brown-black or tan. The cheapest of these has quite thin caps, may be sold with or without stalks, and may well be labelled "fragrant mushrooms", which is the generic term for shiitake mushrooms. Next come the "winter mushrooms" which have thicker caps and taste more fleshy. The most expensive type are called "flower mushrooms". These are the best of the winter mushrooms. The caps are so thick that they crack, revealing the flower pattern that earned them their name. All three have a dusky aroma with a fragrant flavour, which is much intensified by the drying process.

Above: Dried black mushrooms are also known as fragrant mushrooms and are the dried form of shiitake mushrooms.

Culinary uses

These mushrooms are wonderfully versatile as they can be stir-fried, braised, steamed and used in soups. They form an important part of the vegetarians' diet, and are an ideal partner for bamboo shoots, as they offer a harmonious contrast in colour, aroma, flavour and texture. For non-vegetarians, they can be cooked with seafood, poultry and meat, and, of course, other vegetables.

Preparation and cooking techniques

Dried mushrooms must be soaked in water under cover until supple, before use. The best way is to soak in cold water for several hours or overnight, depending on the thickness of the caps. When time is short, they can be soaked in warm water for 30 minutes, but should not be soaked in hot water, as much of the fragrance will be lost. Do not discard the soaking water; it will enrich the flavour of the dish.

After soaking the mushrooms squeeze them dry and discard the stalks, if any. Small mushrooms can be left whole, but larger ones should be halved, quartered or coarsely chopped. The thinner dried mushrooms are usually either thinly sliced or shredded, but thicker ones, particularly the pretty "flower mushrooms" are generally left whole to show off their attractive shape.

Storage

Dried black mushrooms should keep for a very long time (over a year) if stored in a dry, dark and cool place.

Using dried mushrooms

Dried mushrooms have a rich, intense flavour and are a useful store cupboard stand-by for adding to Asian dishes. Once they have been reconstituted they can be stir-fried, braised, steamed and used in soups. Dried mushrooms often require longer cooking than fresh ones.

To reconstitute dried mushrooms, soak them in boiling water for 20–30 minutes, depending on the variety and size of mushroom, until tender. Drain and rinse well to remove any grit and dirt.

WOOD EARS

MANDARIN: *MU'ER;* CANTONESE: *WAN YEE;*
VIETNAMESE: *MOC NHI*

Also known as cloud ears, tree mushrooms or simply dried black fungus, these are widely used in China, Thailand and Vietnam. The dried fungi are thin and brittle, and look like pieces of charred paper.

Aroma and flavour

There is a slightly smoky smell when wood ears are first removed from the packet, but this disappears once they have been soaked. They are almost tasteless, but have an intriguing texture, which is slippery yet crisp.

Culinary Uses

Wood ears are used in stir-frying, braising and soups; the fungus is traditionally paired with dried tiger lily in several Chinese dishes, including the popular hot-and-sour soup.

Preparation and cooking techniques

The fungus expands to six or eight times its volume after soaking, so use plenty of water in a

Right: Wood ears are also known as cloud ears, tree mushrooms or dried black fungus

large bowl. As a guide, a piece of dried fungus that would fit in a tablespoon would require at least 250ml/8fl oz/1 cup water. Cover the bowl and leave the fungus to soak for about 30 minutes, then drain, rinse well and drain again. Discard any hard roots and sandy bits. Do not cut the fungus into small pieces, just separate the larger clumps into individual "ears" in order to preserve the pretty wavy shape.

Storage

Dried fungus will keep almost indefinitely if stored in a dry, cool place; once soaked, it should be kept in clean water in a covered bowl in the fridge. It will keep for 2–3 days.

Left: Silver ears, or dried white fungus

SILVER EARS

MANDARIN: *YINER;* CANTONESE: *PAK MOOK YEE*

Also known as dried white fungus, this earned its Chinese name of "silver ear" partly because of its rarity, and partly because of the high price it fetches on account of its medicinal value. It is regarded as being an excellent tonic, and is also used for the relief of insomnia and lung and liver diseases.

Aroma and flavour

Silver ears do not belong to the same genus as wood ears. Although the texture is similar, white fungus has a sweeter flavour.

Culinary uses

While wood ears are regarded as everyday ingredients, silver ears are reserved for special occasions. Besides being cooked with other vegetables in vegetarian dishes, silver ears are often cooked and then served on their own, as one of the many dishes that comprise a banquet.

Preparation, cooking techniques and storage

Dried silver ears should be prepared, cooked and stored in the same way as dried wood ears.

SEAWEED

KOMBU

CHINESE: *HAIDAI*; JAPANESE: *KOMBU*

Several types of seaweed are used in Asian cooking, especially in Japan and Korea. The most common variety is the giant seaweed known as kelp in English. It is only available in dried form in the West, usually labelled with the Japanese name of kombu or konbu.

Aroma and flavour

Kombu is full of vitamins and minerals, and is particularly rich in iodine. It has a strong "sea" flavour and a crunchy texture.

Culinary uses

This type of seaweed is mainly used in soups in China, but is served poached or stewed as a vegetable in Japan, as well as being used to flavour the fish stock known as dashi.

Left: Kombu has a strong sea flavour.

Dashi

This stock, based on kombu and dried bonito flakes, is the basis of most Japanese soups; it can also be used instead of water in any dish that requires a delicately flavoured stock.

MAKES 800ML/27FL OZ/3½ CUPS

10cm/4in square of kombu
900ml/1½ pints/3¾ cups water
40g/1½oz katsuobushi (dried bonito flakes)

2 Place the pan over a medium heat. Just before the water boils, lift out the seaweed (shred and use for soup).

1 Wipe the kombu with a damp cloth; cut it into 3–4 strips and put in a pan. Pour over the water, making sure that the seaweed is submerged, and soak for an hour.

3 Stir in the bonito flakes, bring to the boil, remove from the heat and leave to stand until the flakes have sunk to the bottom of the pan. Strain through a muslin-lined strainer.

Preparation and cooking techniques

Kombu has a pale powdery covering that contributes to its flavour, so do not wash it off; just wipe the seaweed with a damp cloth, then cut it into pieces of the required size. Soak these in cold water for 45–50 minutes. Both the seaweed and soaking water are used.

Storage

Kombu keeps for a long time if stored in a dry, cool place away from strong light.

NORI

JAPANESE: *NORI*

This is the wafer-thin, dried seaweed that is mainly used as a wrapping for sushi. It is sold in sheets that are dark green to black in colour, and almost transparent in places. The sheet should be grilled lightly on one side for making sushi, or on both sides until crisp if it is to be crumbled and used as a topping. Ready-toasted sheets known as yaki-nori are available from Asian stores. These are seasoned with ingredients such as soy sauce, salt and sesame oil. Ao-nori is dried seaweed that is crumbled so finely it looks like powder.

WAKAME

JAPANESE: *WAKAME*

This young dark-coloured seaweed has a delicate flavour and soft but crisp texture. It is available shredded, fresh (vacuum-packed) or dried, and is used in soups and salads. Dried wakame should be soaked in tepid water for 10–15 minutes until it softens and the fronds turn green. At this stage it should be drained, blanched in boiling water for about 1 minute, then refreshed under cold water and drained again. Use as directed in recipes or cool and chop to use in a salad.

HIJIK

JAPANESE: *HIJIK*

This Japanese seaweed – sometimes called hijiki – is similar to wakame. It is available dried and finely shredded, and should be reconstituted as for wakame.

AGAR-AGAR

CHINESE: *DONGFEN; YANGCAI;*
JAPANESE: *KANTEN*

This is the gelatinous substance obtained from the seaweed known as "rock-flower vegetable" in Chinese. Available from Thai or oriental stores as long dried strips or as a fine white powder sold in tubs, it is a very popular setting agent, especially for vegetarians seeking an alternative to gelatine.

Aroma and flavour

Agar-agar has no aroma and is entirely flavourless, but will absorb the seasonings with which it is prepared for serving.

Culinary uses

Asian cooks sometimes use soaked strips of agar-agar in a salad, just as they would any other form of seaweed, but it is more often used as a

Right: Agar-agar is sold in thick and thin strips and as a powder that is used as a setting agent.

Above: Wakame (in bowl), hijik (on top) and nori seaweeds

Preparation and cooking techniques

To use agar-agar in a salad, soften the strips in lukewarm water for about 20–25 minutes, then drain and dry them on some kitchen paper. Separate the strips and cut them into short lengths. Combine the agar-agar with the other salad ingredients, add a dressing and toss to mix.

To use agar-agar to set a jelly, dissolve it slowly in water over a very low heat, which may take up to 10 minutes. Heat some milk and sugar, with a flavouring such as almond essence, in a separate pan, then mix with the agar-agar solution. Leave the mixture to cool, then chill in the fridge for 3–4 hours until set. Agar-agar varies in strength, so check the packaging to

see how much you should use. As a guide, 5ml/1 tsp powder will set 300ml/½ pint/1¼ cups of liquid.

Storage

Agar-agar, both in strips and in the powdered form, will keep almost indefinitely if stored in a cool, dry place.

FRUIT

DURIAN

CHINESE: *LIU LIAN;* THAI: *THURIAN*

This tropical fruit originated in Malaysia or Borneo, and is very popular in Southeast Asia. Round or oval, it has a dull green shell-like skin covered with pointed spines that turn yellow as the fruit ripens. A typical durian weighs about 2kg/4½lb, but they can grow even larger, up to 4.5kg/10lb.

Aroma and flavour

Durian has a very unpleasant smell, often likened to the stench of raw sewage. The ripe flesh, however, is as delicious as the odour is awful: sweet and creamy, with a hint of strawberries.

Culinary uses

The fruit is eaten raw, and the seeds are often roasted and eaten like nuts.

Preparation

Each fruit consists of three, four or five segments. Using a sharp knife, slit the hard shell of the durian at the segment

Below: A durian and its large seeds

Right: Mangosteen can be eaten on its own or added to a fruit salad.

joints, then press the segments out. Take care not to let the juice drip on to your clothes, as it stains. The soft, creamy flesh can be eaten with a spoon, or puréed, either for serving as a dessert or as an accompaniment to a curry. Some Asian cooks soak the durian segments in coconut milk for 10–12 hours before eating them, as they claim this eliminates the unpleasant smell.

Storage

This is not recommended, as the smell will soon pervade your home, however carefully you store the fruit. When buying, look for perfect, undamaged specimens, and get them home as quickly as possible. Don't attempt to take them on public transport; most carriers ban them!

MANGOSTEEN

CHINESE: *SANZHU GUO;* THAI: *MANG KHUT*

The only thing mangosteens and mangoes share in common, aside from being tropical fruits, is the first five letters of their names. Mangosteens are small, apple-shaped fruits with leathery brown skin that turns purple as they ripen. The flesh looks similar to that of a lychee, but tastes completely different. They are native to South-east Asia and are cultivated in Thailand.

Aroma and flavour

The tough skin surrounds delicious white flesh, which is divided into segments, each with a large seed. The pearly white flesh is fresh and fragrant. Some say it tastes like grapefruit.

Culinary uses

Mangosteens are always eaten raw, but the related kokum, which has a pleasant sour taste, is used as a souring agent in Indian cooking.

Preparation

Cut the fruit in half and remove the segments, taking care not to include any of the dark pink pith. Serve the segments solo or in a fruit salad.

Storage

Mangosteens keep well. If not over-ripe when bought, they should remain in good condition for up to 8–10 days.

LYCHEES

MANDARIN: *LIZHI;* CANTONESE: *LA-EE-TZEE;* THAI: *LIN-CHI*

Indigenous to subtropical areas of southern China and Thailand, lychees grow in clusters on small trees. The ripe fruit is about the size of a small plum, with a beautiful, scaly red skin or "shell". Once this is removed, the pearly white fruit, which surrounds a large inedible seed, is revealed. Fresh lychees are seasonal. When they are not available, canned fruit can be used instead, but it lacks the subtlety of the fresh fruit. Choose the ones in natural juice rather than syrup.

Aroma and flavour

Peeled lychees have a delicious perfume. The flesh has a wonderful, clean taste, somewhat like a grape, but much more scented.

Culinary uses

Lychees and their close relatives, longans, "dragon's eyes", are said to boost fertility. In some parts of China it is traditional, when a young person reaches puberty, to celebrate the event with a meal composed of a young cockerel cooked with dried lychees or longans. On most occasions, however, lychees are eaten fresh, and are good for cleansing the palate after a rich meal. They are also used in fruit salads and for making sorbets.

Preparation

Lychees are very easy to prepare. The brittle skin parts readily, and you can either eat the fruit as is, nibbling the flesh off the stones, or the fruit can be stoned and sliced before being added to a fruit salad or similar dessert.

Storage

Store lychees in the fridge, as they taste best chilled. They will stay fresh for up to a week.

RAMBUTANS

CANTONESE: *HONG MAO TANG;* THAI: *NGO*

These small tropical fruits originated in Malaysia, but they are also grown in the Philippines and Thailand. They belong to the same family as lychees and longans, and they have a similar taste and texture, but look

Above: Canned and fresh rambutans

very different. The reddish-brown skins are covered with fine green-tipped hairs. Inside, the flesh is white, and hides an oblong seed.

Aroma and flavour

Rambutans are not as strongly scented as lychees. The delicate flesh tastes a little sharper.

Culinary uses

Rambutans are usually eaten in the hand, served on the bottom half of the shell, with the top half cut off to expose the flesh. They are used in fruit salads, but are seldom cooked.

Preparation

Make a cut around the equator of the rambutan, then remove half or all the skin. The flesh tends to stick to the seed, so they are more difficult to stone than lychees.

Storage

Like lychees, rambutans are best stored in the fridge, where they will keep for at least a week.

Right: Canned and fresh lychees

Storage

Mangoes are usually picked just before they are ripe, and then they are packed in straw and shipped by air to the West. Fruit that is bought when it is still firm can be ripened at home. One of the easiest ways of doing this is to wrap the mango in newspaper, lay it in a box and cover with more newspaper. Colour is not necessarily an indication of ripeness, but touch is. Ripe fruit will just yield when lightly pressed. Eat mangoes as soon as they are ripe.

Preparing mangoes

Mangoes can be difficult to prepare because they have a large, flat stone that is slightly off-centre, and they are very juicy.

1 Cut off both sides of the fruit in thick slices, keeping as close to the central stone as possible.

2 Scoop the flesh out of the skin using a small spoon. Peel the skin off the remaining central part and slice the fruit off the stone.

MANGOES

CHINESE: *MANG GUO*; THAI: *MA-MUANG*

One of the world's favourite fruits, mangoes originated in India and are now widely cultivated throughout South-east Asia, as well as in other tropical and sub-tropical countries. There are thousands of different varieties. Most are oval in shape, with green, gold or red skin and succulent orange flesh, which can be quite fibrous, although modern varieties are usually smooth and velvety. Canned and dried mangoes are also available.

Aroma and flavour

The aroma of a ripe mango is quite unique. Some people say it reminds them of a pine wood in springtime. The juicy flesh is highly scented and tastes deliciously sweet.

Culinary uses

Apart from being eaten fresh as a fruit, mangoes are used extensively for making chutneys and pickles. Asian cooks also use them in savoury dishes,

Above: A selection of some of the many different varieties of mangoes

and when stir-frying a rich meat such as duck, will often add mango instead of pineapple. Mango ice cream is legendary, and Thai cooks make a wonderful dessert from glutinous rice, coconut milk and mangoes.

Preparation

To prepare a mango for eating, first cut off both sides of the fruit, on either side of the stone, then scoop the flesh out of the skin with a spoon. After that, strip the skin off the remaining central part and suck the stone clean. This may sound rather messy, but in Asia it is the traditional way of eating a mango. If you are fastidious, you can always peel the mango first, slice the fruit off the stone and then slice it neatly. Finally – and this appeals to children – you can cut two large slices from either side of the stone, cross hatch the flesh on the skin, then press the skin down so that the pieces of mango pop up to make a mango "hedgehog".

PAPAYAS

MANDARIN: *FAN MUGUA;* CANTONESE: *MUK GWA;* THAI: *MALAKO*

Papayas – or paw paws as they are sometimes known – are native to tropical America. It was not until 1600 that they were introduced into Asia, but they rapidly became extremely popular so that today they are one of the most common and most important fruits in all tropical and sub-tropical countries.

Papayas can be small and round, but are more often pear-shaped. When ripe, the skin turns from green to yellow, and the flesh, which can be deep salmon pink or glorious orange, becomes soft and juicy. The small grey seeds are not usually eaten, although Asian cooks use them as a garnish.

Aroma and flavour

The flavour of a ripe papaya is sweet and delicately perfumed. It can be sickly, but this can be counteracted by lemon or lime juice. The flesh of underripe papaya is pale green, and nowhere near as sweet.

Culinary uses

In South-east Asia, papaya is eaten both as a fruit and a vegetable. When ripe, the flesh is usually eaten as it is, sometimes with a squeeze of citrus, but it is also used in fruit salads and other desserts. Papayas that are not too ripe can be added to soups, curries or seafood dishes. Unripe green papayas are served raw in vegetable salads, especially in Thailand, and can also be made into pickles. Papaya contains an enzyme called papain, which is an excellent tenderizer. Both the juice and skins are used to tenderize meat.

Preparation and cooking techniques

Slice lengthways in half and scoop out the seeds. To serve papayas raw as a table fruit, slice in wedges, sprinkle with lemon or lime juice, and either cut the flesh off the skin, slicing it into bite-size chunks,

Right: Papayas are one of the most popular tropical fruits.

or provide spoons for scooping. To serve papaya raw in a salad, peel slightly unripe fruit, shred the flesh and combine it with carrots and lettuce or cucumber, then toss with a spicy dressing. Thai cooks often add dried shrimps, which give a salty tang.

Storage

Green papayas are not often available outside their country of origin but, if located, can be kept in a fridge for up to a week. In the West, ripe fruit is much easier to come by. Look for fruit that is yellow all over, and which has a delicate perfume. If the fruit is not quite ripe, check the skin around the stem end and only buy if this is yellow. If it is green, the fruit will never ripen. Fruit that is almost ripe will soften if kept at room temperature for a few days, but should not be left for too long.

Dragon fruit

These brightly coloured fruits are widely grown in Vietnam. They come in pink and yellow varieties. The pink ones are about 10cm/4in long, and are covered with pointed, green-tipped scales. The yellow ones are smaller and look more like prickly pears. The flesh is sweet and refreshing, and is best eaten chilled, sprinkled with a little lemon juice.

NUTS AND SEEDS

PEANUTS

CHINESE: *HUASHENG MI*

Also known as groundnuts or monkey nuts, peanuts are thought to have originated in South America, and were introduced into Asia in the 16th century. Today, peanuts are an important world crop, being rich both in oil (40–50 per cent) and protein (about 30 per cent).

Aroma and flavour

Raw peanuts don't have much of a smell, but once cooked – they are usually roasted – they have a powerful, unmistakable aroma, a crunchy texture and a distinctive flavour.

Culinary uses

Peanuts play an important role in Asian cuisine. The smaller ones are used for making oil, while the larger, less oily nuts are widely eaten, both as a snack food and as ingredients in salads and main courses. In Indonesian and Malayan cooking, roasted peanuts, pounded to a paste, are the basis for satay sauce, as well as for a salad dressing in the classic gado-gado salad.

Above: Raw and shelled peanuts

Preparation and cooking techniques

Strictly speaking, the peanut is not a nut, but a legume. Its outer shell is the dried fibrous pod of the plant, and contains the seeds or "nuts", which in turn are coated with a thin layer of reddish skin. This skin has to be removed before the nut can be used as a food, and the easiest way to do that is to roast or fry the peanuts, then, when they are cool enough to handle, rub off the brittle skins with your fingers. When the nuts are processed commercially, a fan is used for winnowing, or the nuts are left outside to allow the wind to do the job.

Storage

Raw peanuts in their shells will keep for many months if stored properly. Shelled peanuts will only keep for 7–10 days, even if stored in an airtight container.

GINKGO NUTS

CHINESE: *BAIGUO;* JAPANESE: *GINGKO BILOBA*

The ginkgo tree is native to China, and has been grown for many centuries in Japan, where it is called the maidenhair tree.

Aroma and flavour

Ginkgo nuts resemble lotus seeds in appearance and taste, but have a smoother and firmer texture and are somewhat less sweet.

Culinary uses

Ginkgo nuts play an important role in vegetarian cooking in Asia, particularly in China and Japan. They feature in the popular Buddha's delight (a vegetarian casserole) and are used in several Japanese vegetable and rice dishes. When cooked, ginkgo nuts have a viscous texture.

Left: Canned ginkgo nuts

Preparation and cooking techniques

These nuts do not travel well. The flesh inside the shells tends to dry up or rot after a time, so only dried and canned ginkgo nuts are available in the West. Dried nuts need soaking in water for several hours. Drain before adding to stir-fries, casseroles and soups.

Storage

Any unused soaked or canned ginkgo nuts can be stored in fresh water in the fridge for 2–3 days.

ALMONDS

MANDARIN: *XINGREN;*
CANTONESE: *HANG YAHN*

These nuts come from the kernel of a fruit closely related to the apricot, but the fruit of the ripe almond is leathery, dusky green and quite inedible.

Aroma and flavour

Almonds have a unique aroma quite unlike that of any other nut. There are bitter and sweet varieties, both with a pleasant, crunchy texture.

Culinary uses

In Asia, sweet almonds are mostly used as garnishes and in desserts and cakes. Bitter almonds contain prussic acid. They must not be eaten raw, but their essence is distilled and used as a flavouring for sweet dishes.

Above: Shelled
almonds

Preparation and cooking techniques

Whole kernels should be soaked to remove the thin red skin. This is seldom necessary in the West, however, as shelled almonds are readily available, whole, sliced, as thin slivers or ground.

Storage

Almonds have a high fat content, so they become rancid if stored for too long. Keep unopened packets in a sealed container in a cool, dry place, and use within 2–3 months. Nuts bought loose, or in packets that have been opened, should be used as soon as possible.

SESAME SEEDS

CHINESE: *ZHIMA*

The sesame plant probably originated in Africa, but has been cultivated in India and China since ancient times. Today, it is grown all over the world in tropical and sub-tropical countries. Sesame seeds are small, flat and pear-shaped. They are usually white, but can be cream to brown, red or black.

Aroma and flavour

Raw sesame seeds have little aroma and are almost tasteless until they have been roasted or dry-fried, when their nutty aroma becomes very pronounced and their flavour is heightened.

Culinary uses

Sesame seeds are about 50 per cent oil, and processed sesame oil is used in oriental cooking for flavouring. The seeds are used in a number of popular Chinese dishes, most notably in Chinese honeyed apples and bang-bang chicken. They also feature in Singaporean, Malayan Indonesian and Japanese cooking, and are often toasted then sprinkled over salads and other dishes just before serving.

Preparation and cooking techniques

Sesame seeds are frequently roasted before being used. Place them in a wok or pan over a medium heat. They burn readily, so shake the pan constantly to keep them moving and do not leave them unattended at any time. If ground seeds are required, this can be done in a mortar with a pestle, or, as in Korea, between two flat plates. Japanese cooks use a device rather like a pepper mill, which grinds the roasted sesame seeds as finely or as coarsely as needed. The finely ground seeds are called *irigoma*.

Storage

The high oil content means that sesame seeds do not keep well. Store them in a cool, dry place and observe the "use by" dates on packets.

Above: White and black
sesame seeds

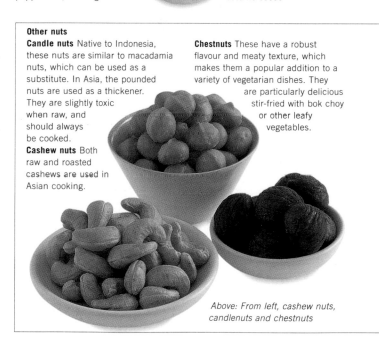

Other nuts
Candle nuts Native to Indonesia, these nuts are similar to macadamia nuts, which can be used as a substitute. In Asia, the pounded nuts are used as a thickener. They are slightly toxic when raw, and should always be cooked.
Cashew nuts Both raw and roasted cashews are used in Asian cooking.

Chestnuts These have a robust flavour and meaty texture, which makes them a popular addition to a variety of vegetarian dishes. They are particularly delicious stir-fried with bok choy or other leafy vegetables.

Above: From left, cashew nuts, candlenuts and chestnuts

BEANCURD/TOFU AND GLUTEN

BEANCURD/TOFU

MANDARIN: *DOUFU;* CANTONESE: *DAU FOO;*
JAPANESE: *TOFU*

Made from soya beans, beancurd (more
commonly known in the West by its
Japanese name tofu) is one of China's
major contributions to the world as a
cheap source of protein. Highly
nutritious and low in fat and sugar, it is
a much healthier food than either meat
or fish, at a fraction of the cost.

The soya bean plant is a legume
that has been cultivated in China for
thousands of years. A number of bean
by-products constitute an important
element in the Chinese diet. Soy sauce
is one of them, and beancurd is
another, as well as miso, the fermented
soya bean paste that is essential to
Japanese cooking. Written records
indicate that fermented bean sauces
were in use well over 2,000 years ago,
but no one knows precisely when
beancurd was invented. All we know for
certain is that it was introduced to
Japan during the Tang dynasty in the
8th century AD, along with Buddhism.

The process of making beancurd is
not unlike making cheese, only much
less time-consuming. The soya beans
are soaked, husked, then pounded with
water to make soya milk. This mixture is
then filtered, boiled and finally curdled
with gypsum.

There are two basic types of fresh
beancurd widely available in the West:
soft or silken tofu (called *kinu* in Japan);
and a firm type, which Japanese
cooks know as *momen.*
Both are creamy-
white in colour
and are either
packed in
water or sold in
vacuum packs.
The firm type is
usually sold in
cakes measuring
about 7.5cm/3in
square and 2.5cm/1in
thick. Also available, but
only from oriental stores, are
marinated beancurd, deep-fried
beancurd and pressed beancurd.

Aroma and flavour

The quality of fresh beancurd is largely
dependent upon the water used to
make it. Good quality beancurd should
smell fresh with a faint, pleasant
"beany" aroma. On its own, it is quite
bland, but the beauty of beancurd is
that its soft, porous texture will absorb
the flavour of any other ingredient with
which it is cooked.

Culinary uses

The nutritional value of beancurd
cannot be stressed too highly. As a
vegetable protein, it contains the eight
essential amino acids plus vitamins A
and B. It is free from cholesterol, and is
regarded as an excellent food for
anyone with heart disease or high blood
pressure. In addition, it is very easy to
digest, so is an ideal food for infants,
invalids and the elderly.

Beancurd is very versatile and,
depending upon the

texture, it can be cooked by almost
every conceivable method, and used
with a vast array of ingredients, both
sweet and savoury.

Preparation and cooking techniques

Soft or silken tofu is mainly steamed or
added to soups, since its light and
delicate texture means that it will
disintegrate if handled roughly. It makes
a refreshing sweet dessert and is also
used to make "ice cream".

Firm beancurd is the most common
type, and also the most popular for
everyday use. Although it has been
lightly pressed, and is more robust than
silken tofu, it still needs to be handled
with care. Having been cut to the
required size and shape – cubes, strips,
slices or triangles – the pieces are
usually blanched in boiling water or
briefly shallow-fried in oil. This hardens
them and prevents them from
disintegrating when stir-fried or braised.
Yaki tofu is beancurd that has been
lightly grilled on both sides.

Because beancurd is bland, it
is important to cook it with
strongly flavoured
seasonings such as
garlic, ginger, spring
onions, chillies, soy
sauce, oyster sauce,
blachan, fermented black
beans, salted

*Above: Clockwise from top, deep-fried
beancurd, silken tofu, and cubes of
fresh beancurd. All these types of tofu
absorb the flavours of the other
ingredients with which they are cooked.*

yellow beans, or sesame oil. Although its primary purpose is as a vegetarian ingredient, beancurd also tastes very good with meat. It is often cooked with either pork or beef, but seldom with chicken. It goes well with fish and shellfish, too. One of the most popular beancurd dishes is the world-famous *ma po doufu* from Sichuan, in which cubed beancurd is first blanched, then braised with minced beef, garlic, spring onions, leeks, salt, Sichuan pepper, rice wine, chilli bean paste, fermented black beans and sesame oil.

Left: Pressed beancurd

Storage

Buy beancurd from an oriental store, if possible. Fresh beancurd submerged in water in a plastic box will keep for several days in the fridge. Vacuum-packed fresh beancurd bought from health food stores and supermarkets will keep for slightly longer, but is unlikely to taste quite as good. Beancurd is also available as a powder mix. This has a long shelf life, so is a useful store-cupboard item.

DEEP-FRIED BEANCURD

MANDARIN: *YOUZHA DOUFU;* CANTONESE: *DAU FOO POK;* JAPANESE: *ABURAGE*

This is fresh, firm beancurd that has been cut into cubes, squares or triangles, then deep-fried until light brown. Deep-fried beancurd has an interesting texture. It puffs up during cooking, and underneath the crispy brown skin the flesh is white and soft. It sucks up seasonings and the flavours of other ingredients like a sponge.

Culinary uses

Deep-fried beancurd can be used in the same way as fresh beancurd in soups, stir-fries, braised dishes or casseroles. As it has been fried in vegetable oil, it is suitable for vegetarian cooking. Non-vegetarians stuff the larger squares or triangles of beancurd with minced pork, chicken, fish and

prawns, then braise them in a sauce. The Japanese version of deep-fried beancurd, known as *aburage,* is a popular addition to a wonderful hotpot called *oden,* which is sold from street stalls during the winter.

Preparation and cooking techniques

Unlike fresh beancurd, which is very delicate, deep-fried beancurd can be handled fairly roughly without disintegrating. Even though the crisp crust is porous, it is best to chop up the larger pieces a little to allow the seasonings to penetrate more easily.

Storage

Cakes of deep-fried beancurd are sold in plastic bags from the chiller or freezer in oriental stores. They usually have a "use by" date stamped on them, and will keep for much longer than uncooked fresh beancurd. They can be frozen for up to a year or more.

PRESSED BEANCURD

MANDARIN: *DOUFU GAN;* CANTONESE: *DAU FOO GONN*

Pressed beancurd is fresh beancurd that has been compressed until almost all the liquid has been squeezed out, leaving a solid block with a smooth texture. It is usually marinated in soy

sauce and seasoned with five-spice powder, so is pale brown on the surface, but white inside.

Culinary uses

Pressed beancurd is cut into thin slices, cubes or fine shreds, then stir-fried with meat and vegetables. It offers a contrast in both texture and flavour when it is combined with other ingredients.

Storage

Pressed beancurd is sold in vacuum-packed plastic bags in oriental stores, and will normally keep for several weeks in the fridge. Check the "use-by" date on the packaging. Do not freeze, as this would alter the texture of the beancurd.

DRIED BEANCURD SKINS

MANDARIN: *FUZHU;* CANTONESE: *FOO PI;* JAPANESE: *YUBA*

Dried beancurd skins are made from soya milk. The process is simple, but requires considerable skill: a large pan of soya milk is gently brought to the boil, the thin layer of skin that forms on the surface is skimmed off with a stick in a single swoop, and this is hung up. When it dries, it forms a flat sheet. Dried beancurd sticks are made by rolling the skin up while still warm, then leaving the sticks to dry.

Culinary uses

Fermented beancurd is either served on its own with rice congee at breakfast, or used as a seasoning in marinating and cooking.

Storage

Fermented beancurd is available in cans and jars from oriental stores. Once opened, store the contents in the fridge.

Below: Fermented beancurd

Above: Dried beancurd skins have no discernible flavour or aroma.

FERMENTED BEANCURD

MANDARIN: *DOUFU NAI*; CANTONESE: *FOO YU*; THAI: *TAO-HOO-YEE*

This is made by fermenting fresh beancurd on beds of rice straw, then drying the curd in the sun before marinating with salt, alcohol and spices. Finally, it is stored in brine in sealed earthenware urns and left to mature for at least six months before being packaged and sold.

Aroma and flavour

Fermented beancurd is definitely an acquired taste. It is no coincidence that it is sometimes referred to as Chinese cheese, because it smells very strong indeed, and the flavour is pretty powerful, too. There are two types of fermented beancurd available in the West: the red type is coloured on the surface only, and the white one can be quite hot and spicy.

Aroma and flavour

Like fresh beancurd, dried beancurd skins have neither aroma nor flavour until they are cooked, when they will absorb the flavour of seasonings and other ingredients.

Culinary uses

The flat skins are used in soups, stir-fries and casseroles, and are sometimes used as wrappers for spring rolls. The sticks are used in vegetarian dishes, and are also cooked with meat in braised dishes and casseroles.

Preparation

Dried beancurd skins need soaking before use: the sheets only require an hour or two, but the sticks need to be soaked for several hours or overnight.

Storage

Dried beancurd sheets and beancurd sticks will keep for a very long time. Store them in their packet or in a sealed plastic bag in a cool and dry place.

Above: Tempeh has a firmer texture than tofu.

TEMPEH

INDONESIAN: *TEMPEH*

This Indonesian speciality is made by fermenting cooked soya beans with a cultured starter.

Aroma and flavour

Tempeh is similar to tofu but has a nuttier, more savoury flavour.

Culinary uses

It can be used in the same way as firm tofu and also benefits from marinating. Its firm texture means that it can be used as a meat replacement.

Storage

Tempeh is available chilled or frozen. Chilled tempeh can be stored in the fridge for up to a week. Frozen tempeh can be left in the freezer for 1 month and should be defrosted before use.

MISO

JAPANESE: *KOME MISO, MUGO MISO AND HACHO MISO*

This thick paste is made from a mixture of cooked soya beans, rice, wheat or barley, salt and water. Miso is left to ferment for up to 3 years.

Aroma and flavour

There are three main types: kome, or white miso, is the lightest and sweetest; medium-strength mugi miso, which has a mellow flavour and is preferred for everyday use; and hacho miso, which is a dark chocolate colour, and has a thick texture and a strong flavour.

Culinary uses

Miso can be used to add a savoury flavour to soups, stocks, stir-fries and noodle dishes, and is a staple food in Asia.

Storage

Miso keeps very well and can be stored for several months, but it should be kept in the fridge once it has been opened.

Left: Hacho miso

Gluten

MANDARIN: *MIANJIN;* CANTONESE: *MING GUN;* JAPANESE: *FU*

Also known as "mock meat", gluten is another source of vegetarian protein. It is made from a mixture of wheat flour, salt and water, from which all the starch has been washed out. What remains is a sponge-like gluten. Its Chinese name literally means "muscle or sinew of flour".

Like beancurd, gluten has no aroma nor flavour of its own, but it has a much firmer texture, and can be shaped, coloured and flavoured to resemble meat, poultry or fish.

Unlike beancurd, which is often cooked with meat and fish, gluten is regarded as a pure Buddhist ingredient, and as such, no non-vegetarian item may be mixed with it. This does not prevent accomplished Asian cooks from using a bit of sleight of hand, however, and gluten is often used with beancurd to produce dishes such as "mock chicken", "mock abalone", "vegetarian duck" or "Buddhist pork" – which are all said to look and taste very much like the real thing.

Although gluten can be made at home, the task is too time-consuming to contemplate. Flavoured and cooked gluten is available in cans from oriental stores. It only needs to be reheated before being served.

Once opened, it will keep in the fridge for up to a week.

DRIED FISH AND SHELLFISH

SALTED FISH

MANDARIN: *YAN YU*; CANTONESE: *GON HAHM YU*

Many different types of fish, both freshwater and saltwater, are salted and cured for general use in South-east Asia. They range from tiny whitebait to large croakers, and they are generally preserved in salt or brine, although some are dried in the sun. In Japan, sun-dried young sardines, known as *niboshi*, are eaten as snacks, and are also used for making stock.

Aroma and flavour

To say that salted fish is an acquired taste is an understatement. It smells so pungent and has such a strong flavour that some people may find it positively disagreeable. It is, however, very popular throughout South-east Asia.

Culinary use

Salted fish has two basic functions. It is either eaten on its own with rice, or used as a seasoning for vegetables and meat in steamed dishes, casseroles or soups.

Preparation and cooking techniques

Soak the salted fish in water before use, to remove the excess salt. Large fish are usually sold without the heads.

Storage

Preserved fish in brine is seldom seen in the West, but salted and dried fish are both available from oriental stores. Salted and dried fish will keep almost indefinitely if stored in a cool, dry place.

DRIED ANCHOVIES

MALAY: *IKAN BILIS*

Dried anchovies, which are known as *ikan bilis*, are a Malayan speciality. For some unknown reason, anchovies are seldom eaten fresh in South-east Asia, they are either used for making fish sauce, or are salted and dried. Fishing for anchovies is a huge industry in Malaysia. Having located the schools of fish with the aid of electronic

Left: Dried anchovies

Above: Bonito flakes or shavings (top) and powder

fish finders and echo sounding equipment, the fishermen haul in their catch and immediately boil the fish in salted water for about 5 minutes. Back on shore, the fish are dried, graded and packed.

Aroma and flavour

Dried anchovies have an overpowering aroma and a very strong flavour.

Culinary uses

Dried anchovies can be used as a flavouring, as an ingredient in a composite dish, or as a snack food. A favourite Malayan recipe involves steaming and filleting the fish, then serving them with a sauce made from preserved black beans that is flavoured with fresh chillies and lime juice and sweetened to taste with sugar. Dried anchovies are also often deep fried until they are crunchy and served either at parties as a snack to eat with drinks, or as a starter. They also make a tasty accompaniment to spicy curries and chicken rendang.

Storage

Dried anchovies will keep for a very long time if stored in a dry and cool place, but make sure that their container is airtight, or you will attract all the neighbourhood cats.

BONITO FLAKES

JAPANESE: *KATSUOBUSHI*

Bonito is the name given to several different kinds of fish in different parts of the world. For instance, the Atlantic bonito is a relative of mackerel, and is known as Spanish mackerel in Europe, while the Pacific bonito is a small tuna, much used in Japanese cooking.

Aroma and flavour

The Pacific bonito has a much stronger flavour than regular tuna, particularly when it is dried.

Culinary uses

In Japan, where dried bonito is widely used, the flakes come in various thicknesses. Fine shavings are one of the main ingredients in the basic stock known as *dashi,* and are also used as a topping or garnish. Powdered bonito flakes are used as a seasoning.

Storage

Dried bonito flakes will keep almost indefinitely if stored in an airtight jar.

DRIED SHRIMPS

MANDARIN: *XIAMI;* CANTONESE: *HA MY;* THAI: *GUNG HAENG*

Dried shrimps are popular throughout Asia, especially in China and Thailand.

They are pale pink in colour, having been boiled before being spread out in the sun to dry. There are several different sizes, from tiny shrimp not much bigger than grains of rice (hence the Chinese name, "sea rice") to large ones, which are still less than 1cm/½in long. The larger ones are usually sold shelled and headless, while the tiny ones are sold whole, heads and all.

Aroma and flavour

Dried shrimps have a very strong smell, so strong that it can be detected through the cellophane bags in which they are sold. The smell dissipates with cooking. The flavour is sharp and salty.

Culinary uses

Because of their strong taste, dried shrimps are usually used as a seasoning rather than as an independent ingredient. They are often used as a garnish in salads and also feature in the popular "eight-treasure stuffing", when they are combined with dried mushrooms, bamboo shoots, glutinous rice and other ingredients.

Preparation and cooking techniques

Dried shrimps must be soaked for an hour or so before use, either in water or rice wine. The soaking liquid is saved and often added to the dish during cooking.

Storage

Dried shrimps keep well in airtight containers if they are stored in a dry, cool place. Their colour is a good indication of freshness as older shrimps tend to fade. Any shrimps that look grey, or

Left: Dried shrimps

Above: Dried scallops

start to turn grey while being stored, will be past their prime. Stored dried shrimps may become a bit moist. If this happens, spread them on baking sheets and dry them briefly in a hot oven.

DRIED SCALLOPS

MANDARIN: *GANBEI;* CANTONESE: *GONG YU CHU*

Another oriental delicacy, dried scallops are very expensive because the most sought-after varieties are so scarce. The Chinese variety known as *conpoy,* for instance, is only found in the inland sea called Po Hai, and then only during a short summer season. The best scallops are round and golden, with a delicate, sweet flavour. Japan produces fine dried scallops, including the variety *aomori.*

Aroma and flavour

Before being dried, scallops are cooked in their shells in boiling water. The flesh is then removed and cleaned. Dried scallops have quite a distinct aroma with a highly concentrated flavour.

Culinary uses

Dried scallops are seldom used on their own, but are combined with other ingredients in soups and stuffings.

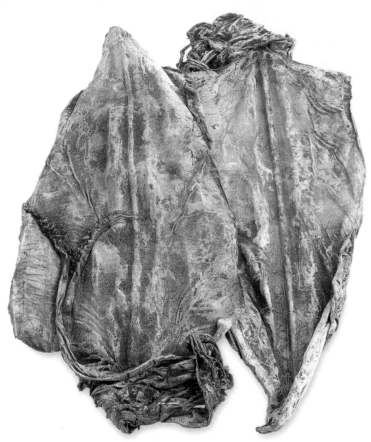

1 Soak the dried squid in warm water for 30 minutes or so, then drain and wash in fresh water.

2 Score the squid on the inside in a criss-cross fashion, then cut it into small pieces.

Above: Dried squid has a subtle fishy aroma, but a strong flavour.

Dried and fresh scallops are sometimes used in the same dish. Dried scallops are the classic garnish for crispy seaweed, but when this dish is served in Chinese restaurants overseas, ground fried fish is often used as a substitute.

Preparation and cooking techniques

The scallops must be soaked in boiling water for at least an hour before use, then drained.

Storage

For some inexplicable reason, dried scallops seem to be available only in large boxes in the West. Should you acquire any, transfer them to jars, close the lids tightly and store them in a cool, dry place. They will keep indefinitely.

DRIED SQUID

MANDARIN: *YOUYU*; CANTONESE: *YOW YU*

In inland China and other parts of Asia that are far from the coast, where fresh seafood was for a long time unobtainable, dried squid and cuttlefish have always been regarded as delicacies.

Aroma and flavour

Dried squid is pale brown in colour and has a subtle fishy aroma, but a very strong taste. Some people find the texture rather tough when compared to fresh squid, but others like the chewiness of the dried version.

Culinary uses

In Asia, dried squid is mainly used in soups or meat stews. The stronger texture and flavour provides an interesting contrast to fresh squid, and the two are often stir-fried together in a popular dish that is known as "two-coloured squid-flowers".

Preparation and cooking techiques

Before using them for cooking, dried squid must be soaked in warm water for at least 30 minutes, then drained and cleaned in fresh water. If the dried squid is to be stir-fried, it is the normal practice to score the inside of the flesh in a criss-cross pattern, then cut it into small pieces. Cooking causes the cuts to open up so that each piece of squid resembles an ear of corn, which is how they came to be called "squid flowers".

Storage

Dried squid will keep almost indefinitely if they are wrapped tightly and stored in a dry, cool place.

FISH MAW

CHINESE: *YU DU*

Fish maw is the swim bladders or stomachs of certain types of large fish and eels, which have been dried in the sun for several days, then deep-fried. It is considered a delicacy in both China and Thailand.

Aroma and flavour

Fish maw has little aroma, nor does it have a distinctive flavour.

Culinary uses

Fish maw is mainly valued for its texture, which is slippery.

Preparation and cooking techniques

The maws must be soaked in a large bowl of cold water for 24 hours before use. They will float at first, so will need to be kept submerged with the aid of a plate or dish. As they absorb the water, the maws will swell to four times the original size and slowly sink to the bottom of the bowl. Before use, drain but do not dry the maws, then slice or cube them as required.

Above: Fish maw

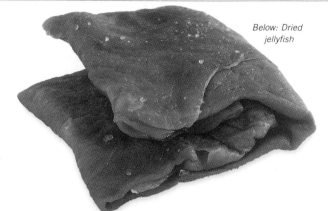

Below: Dried jellyfish

Dried jellyfish

Sheets of dried edible jellyfish are sold in plastic bags in some Chinese stores. This Chinese delicacy is valued for its crunchy yet elastic texture. To prepare, soak the sheets in cold water for several hours, changing the water frequently, and squeezing the jellyfish each time to get rid of as much of the fishy smell as possible. Drain, give the jellyfish sheets a final squeeze to remove the excess water, then cut them into strips. Strips of dried jellyfish are often added to a stir-fry, but they must be tossed in at the last moment; if they are over-cooked, they will become rubbery.

Left: Dried sea cucumber, which is actually a type of sea slug and not a vegetable at all.

Dried sea cucumber Sold as *iriko*, *trepang* or *bêche-de-mer*, this is not a vegetable, but a marine animal, also known as a sea slug. Before use, dried sea cucumber must be soaked in cold water for at least 24 hours, during which time it will double in bulk and become quite gelatinous. It is mainly used in soups, stews and braised dishes.

PRESERVED MEATS AND EGGS

CHINESE SAUSAGES/ WIND-DRIED SAUSAGES

MANDARIN: *XIANG CHANG;* CANTONESE: *LOP CHONG*

Although these are always described as Chinese sausages, wind-dried sausages are made throughout South-east Asia, and are widely available in the West. There are basically two types: a pink and white sausage, which is made from pork and pork fat, and a darker sausage, in which the pork is mixed with duck liver. The sausages are about 15cm/6in long and about 2cm/¾in wide, and are sold in pairs, tied together with string.

Aroma and flavour

The dried sausages do not have any aroma, but as soon as they are cooked, they become really fragrant and taste deliciously sweet.

Culinary uses

Chinese sausages are very versatile. They can be eaten on their own, combined with milder meats such as chicken, or used as the main ingredient in a vegetable dish.

Preparation and cooking techniques

Unlike salami, Chinese sausages must be cooked before eating them. The best way of cooking them is to cut them diagonally into thin slices, then steam them on top of rice for 10 minutes or so. Alternatively, the whole sausage can be steamed for 10 minutes, then skinned and sliced before adding to dishes such as fried rice.

Storage

As the sausages are cured and contain preservatives, they will keep for several months in the fridge, and almost indefinitely in the freezer.

Right: Chinese sausages are popular throughout South-east Asia.

Above: Pork crackling

PORK CRACKLING

MANDARIN: *SAI YUDU;* CANTONESE: *JA YUHK PEI*

Also known as chicaron, pork crackling is made from pork rind that has been deep-fried, forming crisp puffy crackers. It is served as a crunchy contrast alongside curries, or sliced in salads.

Aroma and flavour

The deep-fried rind has a meaty aroma with a subtle flavour. It has a very interesting firm yet spongy texture that absorbs other strongly flavoured ingredients.

Wind-dried belly pork

This is a Chinese speciality, found principally in Hunan province but available all over China. It must be cooked before eating. Wind-dried belly pork can be bought in oriental stores.

Culinary uses

Pork crackling is used in soups, stews, hot pots and casseroles.

Preparation

Pork crackling is simply sliced if it is to be used as a crunchy topping for salads, otherwise it needs to be soaked before use, partly to soften it and partly to rid it of excess fat. It is usually soaked in hot water for about 35 minutes before being drained and chopped.

Storage

Pork crackling should keep for several months if well wrapped and stored in a cool, dry place. It will become rancid if kept for too long.

PRESERVED EGGS

MANDARIN: *YANDAN; PIDAN;* CANTONESE: *HAHAM DON; PEI DON*

In China, and among the Chinese communities throughout South-east Asia, preserved eggs are a very popular delicacy. There are two main types, and both use duck eggs. This is partly because duck eggs are bigger and have a stronger flavour than hen's eggs, but also because the yolk of a duck egg contains more fat than a hen's egg. The more common type, much favoured in southern China, is the salted duck egg. The other, which has more universal appeal, is the famous thousand-year-old egg.

Both types of preserved egg are made by a similar method; it is the materials used in the process that are different. Basically, salted eggs are made by coating raw duck eggs in a salt and mud paste, then rolling them in rice husks until they are completely covered. At this stage the eggs are packed into an earthenware urn, which is tightly sealed and stored in a cool, dark place for 30–40 days. Thousand-year-old eggs are nothing like as old as their name suggests. They are raw duck eggs that have been covered with a mixture of wood ash and slaked lime and left for up to a hundred days. By the time they are used, the egg whites will have turned to pale brown jelly and the yolks will be creamy and tinged green.

Aroma and flavour

The two types of preserved egg smell and taste quite different. As might be expected, the former are quite salty. Thousand-year-old eggs taste milder, but still have a definite aroma and flavour.

Above: The solid whites and yolks of thousand-year-old eggs are eaten raw. The eggs only require peeling.

Culinary uses

Salted eggs must be cooked. They are often eaten on their own, or used as part of the filling in cakes for festivals. Thousand-year-old eggs need no cooking. Sliced and seasoned with soy sauce and sesame oil, they are often served as a starter, or chopped and added to congee and eaten at breakfast time. They can also be used in a delicious omelette, with pork and fresh hen's eggs.

Preparation and cooking techniques

Both types of egg must have their outer coating removed and then they should be thoroughly washed. Salted eggs can then be boiled or steamed before removing the shells. The whites and yolks of thousand-year-old eggs will have solidified, so all that is required is to carefully remove the shell before cutting the eggs into quarters or eighths for serving.

Storage

Since these eggs are preserved, they should keep for a long time in the fridge. The salted eggs will keep for about a month, and the thousand-year-old eggs will keep for 4–6 months.

Left: Throughout Asia thousand-year-old eggs (front) and salted duck eggs (back) are a very popular delicacy.

POULTRY

CHICKEN

The chicken is a descendant of a South-east Asian jungle fowl that was domesticated over 4,500 years ago. Today chicken features in almost every cuisine. Its universal popularity is due to the fact that the flesh combines happily with a huge variety of different ingredients. Nowhere is this more amply illustrated than in Asia, where it is used in soups, salads, stir-fries, curries, roasts and braised dishes. Every part of the bird is utilized, including the liver, gizzard, heart and even the feet, which are used to make a delicious stew in South-east Asia.

Preparation and cooking techniques

Chicken can be cooked whole, jointed, or taken off the bone and chopped or cut into thin strips – this is the usual practice if the meat is to be stir-fried. In China, chicken breasts on the bone are sometimes cut into as many as 20 pieces before being stir-fried. The ability of the Chinese to pick up these

Game birds

Small game birds are eaten in China and South-east Asia, but most are caught in the wild. Only quail and pigeon are farmed.

tiny pieces of chicken with chopsticks and to remove the meat from the bone in the mouth is a marvel of dexterity.

Serving meats and other foods in manageable morsels is the norm in Asia, where knives are viewed as weapons, and therefore inappropriate for such enjoyable communal activities as meals. Chopsticks are widely used, except in Thailand, where it is more common to find a spoon and fork at each table setting.

In Japan, chicken is the most important meat on the menu, second only to fish in terms of popularity. Chicken breast is the favourite cut, largely because it cooks so quickly and remains beautifully tender in dishes such as the famous *yakitori* or *teriyaki*. Skinless, boneless chicken breasts are readily available in Japan, unlike in the rest of Asia, where it is more usual for cooks to buy chickens whole, as portions are regarded as wasteful, or simply as too expensive.

Throughout the East, frugality is a virtue, so one chicken might be used in three dishes: the breasts sliced in strips for a stir-fry; the rest of the meat braised in a red cooked dish or a curry; and the carcass used to make stock.

The skill that is exhibited by oriental cooks with the simplest equipment is testament to their creative love of food. Using a cleaver and a small sharp knife, a chicken can be chopped into appropriate portions in no time at all.

DUCK

Ducks symbolize happiness and fidelity, which doubtless contributes to their popularity in the Chinese cuisine. Duck is central to celebratory meals, and is served in countless imaginative ways. At Chinese New Year, for instance, duck is an essential part of every banquet.

How to joint a chicken
This method will give you eight good-sized portions of chicken.

1 Place the chicken breast side up on a chopping board. Ease one of the legs away from the body, and using a sharp knife make an incision to reveal the ball of the thighbone as you pull the leg further away from the body. When the thigh socket is visible, cut through the bone to release the drumstick and thigh in one piece. Repeat with the other leg.

2 Trim off the end of the leg bone, then locate the knee joint and cut the leg portion in half at this joint. Repeat with the other chicken leg.

3 Cut through the breastbone so that the carcass is in two halves. Cut and separate each breast and wing from the backbone.

4 Cut both of the wing and breast pieces into two portions.

COOK'S TIPS
• Use the backbone to make stock, adding onion, celery and a piece of bruised root ginger if appropriate.
• If more pieces of chicken are required, say for stir-fries, the portions can be further divided. Deft oriental cooks will cut the breast and wing portions into as many as ten pieces, the legs into four pieces and the thighs into six pieces.

Right: In Asia, every part of the chicken is used – even the feet.

Duck is also popular in Vietnam,Thailand and Indonesia, but is seldom served in Japan.

Preparation and cooking techniques

The most famous duck dish has to be Peking duck. The classic way of making this universally popular restaurant dish involves hanging the prepared birds in a windy place to dry before roasting them in a special oven. At one time only the skin was eaten, but it is now more usual to eat the succulent meat as well. This is wrapped in a Mandarin pancake which has been spread with a little plum sauce and sprinkled with a few pieces of shredded spring onion and slivers of cucumber. This dish is so popular that is now possible to buy packages of Peking duck, with all the trimmings, in the West.

The Chinese technique for preparing duck for roasting involves pricking the skin lightly all over with a fork, placing the bird on a trivet in the sink, then pouring a kettle of freshly boiled water over the top. The bird is then drained well, and the cavity wiped with kitchen paper, before being suspended from duck hooks or butcher's hooks and left to dry overnight. Once the bird is dry, the skin is sprinkled with a little salt. The bird is then placed on a trivet in a roasting tin and roasted in a hot oven until the skin is quite crisp and golden brown and the bird is fully cooked.

If the duck is to be jointed the same procedure can be used as for chicken.

COOK'S TIP

To make duck sauce to serve with Peking duck, heat 30ml/2 tbsp sesame oil in a small saucepan. Add 90ml/ 6 tbsp yellow bean sauce and 30ml/2 tbsp soft light brown sugar and stir until smooth. Leave to cool before serving.

Right: An oven-ready duck

MEAT

PORK

This is as popular as chicken in China and in other parts of Asia with large Chinese communities. Like chicken, it blends happily with a wide range of ingredients, from vegetables to shellfish, and is equally at home with salted and pickled foods.

Wherever there are Muslim communities, however, pork is off limits and either beef or lamb is served instead. This is the case throughout Malaysia, the only exception being the Nonya style of cooking. This came about because of the intermarriage of Chinese merchant men with Malayan women who then started to cook pork dishes for their husbands. Nonya cooking is popular in Singapore, the west coast of Malaysia around Malacca and on the island of Penang.

Pork seldom features in Indonesian cuisine, except where cooked by members of the Chinese communities on the thousands of islands of the archipelago. Bali is an exception. The population of this island are mainly Hindu and therefore pork is permissible and widely used.

Throughout Asia, therefore, the choice of meat is greatly influenced by religious beliefs and habits. Almost all Chinese except those who have converted to Islam love pork. Thais find the smell of lamb and mutton offensive; and Indians would never touch beef, because for them the cow is sacred. Poultry has none of these taboos.

Preparation and cooking techniques

For stir-frying, fillet, lean leg or belly are the preferred cuts, along with the meaty parts of chops or spare ribs. The meat is cut into thin shreds so that it responds to really quick cooking over high heat, which is economical in the use of fuel.

For casseroles and braised dishes shoulder, spare ribs or belly pork might be used, and the meat is often cooked for so long that it forms a luscious jelly-like mixture.

OTHER MEATS

Beef has only relatively recently been eaten in China and Asia, because cattle were considered beasts of burden and highly valued as such. The buffalo, too, has always been used widely, mainly in the paddy fields to plough the land prior to planting by hand. Beef and lamb are traditionally eaten only in the north of China and in places such as Malaysia where there are Muslim communities. However, because of the proximity of Beijing to the northern provinces and the number of Chinese Muslim restaurants in the capital, lamb and beef are becoming increasingly popular there, too.

Lamb is cooked in the famous Mongolian hotpot, while beef is used in many different types of recipes, mainly as a substitute for pork. It is generally thinly sliced and used for dishes where a quick method of cooking such as stir-frying is required. Because it has a stronger flavour than pork, it works best in dishes that contain aromatic flavouring ingredients, such as garlic and onions.

Above: Lean leg steaks, fillet and spare ribs are the preferred cuts of pork.

FISH

There is an old Thai saying that suggests that all is well when "there is fish in the water and rice in the field". The main source of protein in the Thai diet is fish, which is hardly surprising when you take a look at the map and see the immense coastline in addition to the rivers, canals, lakes and flooded paddy fields. Along these waterways local people catch their daily supply of fish using simple fishing poles or nets. The fish is steamed, grilled with local spices or herbs, served in soups or curries, or added to salads or omelettes.

The Cantonese word for fish is "yu" which sounds the same as the word for abundance or bounty. A whole fish is traditionally served at the Chinese New Year banquet as a symbol of hope that the family will enjoy a plentiful supply of food during the coming year. Serving a fish whole, as opposed to cutting it into portions, has great appeal in Asia, as the fish is aesthetically pleasing and complete. Also, by cooking the fish whole the juices are retained and the prized morsel that is the fish cheek can be served to the guest of honour.

Fish – nature's bounty – is exploited and enjoyed all over the East. With a coastline of over three thousand miles China has an abundant and varied supply of saltwater fish, some of which are familiar to Westerners, such as bass and sea bass, halibut, mackerel, sea bream, sole, plaice, tuna, cod, salmon, sardines and herring. China also has majestic rivers and lakes, which are a source of freshwater fish, including the ubiquitous carp.

Indonesia, the Philippines and Japan are all island nations, so it is not surprising that fish plays an important role in their cuisines. This is especially so in Japan, where an early moratorium on meat eating was one of the factors

Above: Freshwater carp, mackerel and grey mullet

that led to the Japanese expertise in preparing this popular food. Sashimi – very fresh fish that is finely sliced and served raw – is a delectable treat that is now appreciated well beyond the shores of the country that invented it. Trout, mackerel, tuna, salmon and herring are popular in Japan, as well as more exotic varieties, such as parrot fish or pomfret.

The most important requirement when buying and preparing is that it be as fresh as possible. This goes for all of Asia, but particularly Japan.

Buying fish

When buying fresh fish, the following indicators should be considered:
• The eyes of the fish should be bright and clear, not sunken.
• Gills should be clean and bright red/coral in colour.
• The skin should be firm and fresh with a sheen and, when held, the fish should feel almost springy, as if it could swim away at any moment.
• Freshness can also be detected in the smell. It is difficult to disguise the odour of a fish that is past its prime.

Cooking fish

Steaming and simmering in clear stock are typical Asian cooking methods, along with deep-frying, pan-frying, stir-frying and braising.
Steaming Choose a very fresh whole fish. It should not be too large (about 675g/1½ lb). Rub the skin with salt and scatter the fish with shredded fresh root

ginger. Pour over a mixture of Chinese rice wine, soy sauce and sugar, then steam immediately over rapidly boiling water. For the best results remove the fish from the steamer when the fish is almost, but not absolutely cooked. The flesh should have just begun to flake when tested with the tip of a sharp knife, but should still be beautifully moist. Serve with the cooking juices poured over.

Clear simmering This method is usually reserved for larger fish (about 1.5kg/ 3lb). Use a fish kettle, if you have one. Pour in 1.75 litres/3 pints/7½ cups water and add salt to taste. Slice a 4cm/1½in piece of root ginger and add the slices to the kettle. Bring the water to the boil. Meanwhile slip a wide strip of foil under the fish to act as a strap. Lift the fish into the kettle, placing it on the trivet. Allow the water to return to

Right: Snapper, parrot fish and pomfret

the boil, then lower the heat and simmer for about 4 minutes. Lower the heat again, until the water barely bubbles, and cook the fish for 6–8 minutes. Lift the fish out of the fish kettle and let it drain before transferring it to a heatproof serving dish. Heat 75ml/5 tbsp groundnut oil and pour this over the hot fish to complete the cooking. This is a finish also used in Vietnamese cuisine, but they would scatter the fish with shredded spring onion before pouring over the hot oil.

Frying Fish can be stir-fried, deep fried or pan-fried, and whichever method is used, the fish is always cooked quickly to retain its shape and flavour.

Braising Used for whole fish, which is first fried in garlic and ginger oil. Soy sauce, Chinese mushrooms and other flavourings are added, then the pan is covered tightly and the fish is cooked very briefly.

TYPES OF FISH

Carp A freshwater fish that is believed to have originated in Asia thousands of years ago. It is extensively farmed and thrives in ponds, lakes and flooded paddy fields. There are several varieties. Ask the fishmonger to remove the large scales and strong dorsal fins. The flesh is meaty and moist. Bake carp whole. Like grey mullet, it needs a stuffing with a distinctive flavour.

Cod A handsome fish with greenish bronze skin dappled with yellow, cod can vary in size from 1kg/2¼lb to 30kg/66lb. When properly cooked the flesh is moist and will break into large flakes. It is ideal for grilling, baking or frying, and is excellent in fish curries, but only add the cubes of pearly white fish at the very end of cooking so that they keep their shape.

Grey mullet This fish has dark stripes along the back, lots of thick scales and a heavy head. The flesh is soft and rather coarse but responds well to distinctive flavours. Try it baked, with a stuffing of minced pork and prawns with ginger and spring onion or chopped Chinese mushrooms, or moisten it with fish sauce and steam it.

Halibut This is a rather chunky flatfish and can reach an enormous size. It has a brownish skin on one side and is pearly white underneath with two eyes on the bridge of the snout. The smaller type, called a chicken halibut, weighs under 1.5kg/3lb and is ideal for poaching or baking.

Mackerel Mackerel and bonito are from the same family. The fish is easy to recognize, thanks to the wavy dark blue markings which run part of the way down to a silvery green side and pale underbelly. The inside of the mouth is black. Mackerel is an oily fish, with soft, pinkish flesh, and is ideal for grilling or poaching with miso. Serve mackerel with wedges of lemon or lime. It is also excellent in a *laksa* or a Thai fish soup.

Parrot fish Either blue or brightly coloured, these are striking to look at and delicious to eat.

Plaice Easy to recognize, this flatfish has dark brown skin with orange spots and a white underside. The flesh is soft and moist. Cook plaice whole, either deep-fried or poached. If filleted, make a stock from the bones with bruised ginger, onion and seasoning.

Pomfret Held in high regard by Malay and Thai cooks, the pomfret is a fisherman's dream as it is very easy to net. So easy that at one stage these fish were almost fished out. A type of flatfish, pomfret is silver grey with a pearly white underside. The ideal way to preserve the delicate flavour of this fish is to steam it with a few simple flavourings, such as ginger, spring onion, light soy sauce and seasoning. It is good grilled and fried, too.

Salmon Often called the king of fish, the finest wild salmon makes delicious sashimi. Farmed salmon makes a very reasonable and good buy for a vast array of cooked dishes. The skin on a salmon's back is steely blue going down to a silver body. The flesh is oily, an attractive shade of pink, and firm. It is best either clear simmered or poached in a fish kettle or wrapped in foil and baked. Cutlets can be barbecued and served with Thai salad or used to make the Filipino dish, escabeche.

Sea bass The family of sea bass also includes the groupers (sometimes called garoupas). Sea bass is silver in colour with a dark back and white underbelly. The flesh is delicate in flavour and holds its shape when cooked. The fish can be grilled, steamed, baked or barbecued whole, or cut into fillets or steaks before being cooked. It is expensive but worth it.

Sea bream Look for the gilt head with a gold spot on each cheek and squat compact body. Sea bream must be scaled before being cooked. The flesh is rather coarse but remains moist if not overcooked. Slash each side two or three times so that the thicker part of the fish will cook more evenly. Sea bream is best baked whole in an oiled or buttered foil parcel with ginger, spring onion and seasoning. It is good served with a sweet and sour sauce.

Above: Tuna steaks and salmon cutlets

Snapper The red snapper is perhaps the best known but there other colours, too, such as grey, silver and even a silver-spotted grey. The red colour is quite distinctive. The fish has large eyes and very strong dorsal fins which should be removed before cooking. The flesh is moist and well flavoured. Small to medium snappers are good for steaming or baking whole.

Sole Another member of the flatfish family, sole has rough brown skin on top and a long lozenge-shaped body. The flesh has superb texture and a delicate flavour. Sole is best grilled or fried whole. It can be sold filleted, in which case ask for the bones to make stock for a fish soup.

Squid Asian cooks are fond of squid. In the West, this cephalopod usually comes ready cleaned, but if you should you come across squid in the unprepared state here is what to do: Pull the tentacles out from the body sac. Squeeze the tentacle in the centre gently to remove the hard central bone or "beak". Trim the tentacles from the head and set aside. Using fingers pull the quill and innards from the body cavity and discard. Pull off the mottled outer skin, it should come away quite easily. Wash the squid well inside and out. It is now ready for stuffing. When it is two thirds full, pop the tentacles back into the top of the sac. Secure the tentacles and the top of the squid body with a cocktail stick.

If the squid are to be stir-fried, further preparation will be necessary: Slit the sac from top to bottom and turn it inside out. Flatten it on a board and score the inside surface lightly with a knife, pressing just hard enough to make a criss-cross pattern. Cut lengthways into ribbons. These will curl when cooked.

Tuna These enormous fish are the big brothers of the mackerel family. Tuna swim enormous distances at speed and this causes the muscles to fill with blood, which explains the deep red colour of the fresh fish. The skipjack and the albacore are much sought after by the Japanese for making **sashimi** and **sushi.** When grilling or barbecuing tuna, marinate the fish first and then baste it to keep it moist throughout the cooking. It is also good pan-fried.

SHELLFISH

Asian cooks have access to a wonderful assortment of shellfish, not only from the ocean, but also – in the case of crabs and shrimps – from freshwater lakes, rivers and canals. In Asia it is considered essential that shellfish be as fresh as possible when cooked. This isn't always possible for the Western cook, who often has no option but to resort to using good quality frozen shellfish. In this case, the shellfish should be thawed slowly, and dried before being cooked. The cooking period should be kept to a minimum to preserve the delicate flavour and texture of the shellfish. In Asia, favoured cooking methods for shellfish are steaming, deep-frying and stir-frying, but they are also used in soups, and made into dishes such as crab cakes.

Abalone This large shellfish has a particularly pretty shell, lined with what looks like mother-of-pearl. The flesh of abalone can be tough, and it is usually beaten to tenderize it before cooking. Frozen abalone is available from some oriental markets, and it Is also possible to buy canned abalone. This is yellow brown in colour and has a savoury flavour. The texture tends to be rubbery, so canned abalone is seldom served solo, but is usually combined

Above: Mussels and clams

with other ingredients. The can juices can be used in soups and sauces. Dried abalone is an expensive and much sought-after delicacy.

Clams There are many different types of clam. In Japan, the giant clam and the round clam are both used for making sushi, and in China clams with black bean sauce are a favourite treat. When buying clams, check that none of the shells are broken. Wash them well in running water, then leave in salt water before steaming for 7–8 minutes or until the shells open. Serve clams simply, with a dipping sauce

Above: Canned abalone

Mussels and Clams in Coconut Cream

Mussels and clams can be steamed, but here they are cooked Thai-style in coconut cream and flavoured with lemon grass, kaffir lime leaves and Thai green curry paste.

SERVES 4–6

1.75 kg/4 – 4¹/₂lb mussels
450g/1lb baby clams
120ml/4fl oz/¹/₂ cup dry white wine
1 bunch spring onions, chopped
2 lemon grass stalks, chopped
6 kaffir lime leaves, chopped
10ml/2 tsp Thai green curry paste
200ml/7fl oz/scant 1 cup coconut cream
30ml/2 tbsp chopped fresh coriander
salt and ground black pepper

1 Scrub the mussels, pull off the beards and remove any barnacles. Discard any mussels that are broken or which do not close when tapped sharply. Wash the clams thoroughly.

2 Put the wine in a large saucepan with the spring onions, lemon grass, lime leaves and curry paste. Simmer gently until the wine has almost evaporated. Add the mussels and clams to the pan, cover tightly and steam the shellfish over a high heat for about 6 minutes, until they open.

3 Using a slotted spoon, transfer the mussels and clams to a heated serving bowl and keep hot. Discard any shellfish that remain closed. Strain the cooking liquid into a clean pan and simmer to reduce to about 250ml/8fl oz/1 cup.

4 Stir in the coconut cream and coriander, with salt and pepper to taste. Heat through. Pour the sauce over the mussels and clams.

is often pan-fried or cooked in a pot of rice where it releases a delicious, delicate flavour.

Lobster This luxury shellfish is usually served as a restaurant dish. To cook a live lobster, put it in a pan of ice cold water, cover the pan tightly and bring the water to the boil. The shell will turn bright red and the flesh will be tender and succulent when the lobster is cooked. If you buy a ready-cooked lobster the tail should spring back into a curl when pulled out straight. One of the best ways of eating lobster is with a simple dip of soy sauce with grated ginger.

Scallops Prized for their tender, sweet flesh, scallops are popular throughout Asia. The delicate flesh needs the briefest possible cooking. An excellent way of cooking scallops is to marinate them in a mixture of Chinese rice wine, sugar and soy sauce for 30 minutes, then steam them with the marinade and some slivers of ginger and spring onion.

Above: Lobster and scallops

based on hoisin sauce, plum sauce or soy sauce with ginger. Clams are also very good in soups.

Mussels Another shellfish that is widely used in oriental cooking. Farmed mussels are now readily available and have the advantage that they are usually relatively free of barnacles. They are generally sold in quantities of 1kg/2¼lb, sufficient for a main course for two or three people. Look for good-size specimens with glossy shells. Discard any that are not closed, or which fail to shut when tapped. Use the back of a short stout knife to scrape away any barnacles, pull away the hairy "beards", then wash the shellfish thoroughly. The best way to cook mussels is to steam them in a small amount of flavoured liquor in a large lidded pan for 3–4 minutes until the shells open. Use finely chopped ginger, lemon grass, a few torn lime leaves and some fish sauce to add flavouring to the mussels.

Crabs are eaten with great relish all over the East. There are many different species which are exclusive to Asia. Travellers to Thailand and Hong Kong will doubtless have seen – and enjoyed – blue swimming crabs. This species obligingly moults its shell so that the crab can be eaten whole. The meat

Below: Blue swimming crabs

Left: Cooked prawns

Fantail or phoenix prawns

This way of serving prawns comes from China. The cooked prawns, with their bright red tails, are supposed to resemble the legendary phoenix, which is a symbol of dignity and good luck. Large prawns are used.

1 Remove the heads from the prawns and peel away most of the body shell. Leave a little of the shell to keep the tail intact.

2 Make a tiny incision in the back of each prawn and remove the black intestinal cord.

3 Hold the prepared prawns by the tails and dip them lightly in seasoned cornflour, and then in a frothy batter before cooking them in hot oil until the tails, which are free from batter, turn red.

Shrimps and prawns Both shrimps and prawns can be caught in either fresh water or the sea. The names tend to be used indiscriminately in Asia. Shrimps can be small or large and the same holds good for prawns. Buy fresh raw shellfish where possible, choosing specimens that are a translucent grey colour tinged with blue. If using frozen shrimps and prawns, it is preferable to buy raw shellfish, thaw them slowly and dry them well before using. Further preparation will depend upon the chosen recipe. The shells may be left on or removed, or the shrimps or prawns may be shelled, with the tails left intact.

Left: Raw prawns

Butterfly prawns

Prawns prepared this way cook quickly and curl attractively.

1 Remove the heads and body shells of the prawns, but leave the tails intact. Pull out the intestinal cords with tweezers.

2 Make a cut through the belly of each prawn.

3 Gently open out the two halves of the prawn so that they will look like butterfly wings.

Above: Garlic

GARLIC

MANDARIN: *SUAN;* CANTONESE: *SUEN;*
THAI: *KRATIAM*

Garlic is a member of the lily family, which is the same genus as leeks and onions. It is believed to have originated in Asia, and is mentioned in Chinese texts that date back over 3,000 years. The ancient Egyptians valued it for food and also accorded it a ceremonial significance. Garlic's curative qualities are well documented, and in many cultures it is used to ward off evil.

Aroma and flavour

There are several varieties of garlic, from tiny heads to the aptly named elephant garlic. The colour of the skin varies from white through to pink and purple, and the flavour can be anywhere from mild to extremely pungent. The most common variety In the Far East has a purple skin, a distinctive aroma and a fairly strong flavour with a hint of sweetness. In South-east Asia, cooks use a miniature variety of garlic. There are only four to six cloves in each bulb, and both the aroma and the flavour are much more concentrated. Thai cooks favour small garlic bulbs whose cloves have such thin skins that it is seldom necessary to remove them for cooking. The cloves are simply smashed with a cleaver, then added to the pan, where the skins dissolve to become part of the dish.

Culinary uses

Garlic forms a trinity of flavours with spring onion and ginger in thousands of dishes in Chinese cooking, particuarly in Beijing and Sichuan. It is a basic ingredient in much of Asia, including Korea, but is less popular in Japan, where it is used mainly for medicinal purposes. Vietnamese cooks use a great deal of garlic, and in Thailand a mixture of crushed garlic, coriander root and pepper is the foundation of many dishes. Garlic is an essential ingredient in the famous Thai curry pastes, too. Throughout Asia, garlic is also used to flavour oil for frying, partly because of the aromatic flavour it imparts, and also because it cuts down on the "oiliness".

Raw garlic is often used in dips, marinades and dressings.

Preparation and cooking techniques

Except in a few rare instances, when whole cloves of garlic are roasted or packed inside a chicken, garlic is always peeled before use. One of the easiest ways of doing this is to place it on a chopping board and crush it with the flat blade of a Chinese cleaver. The skin will separate from the flesh, and can easily be removed before the garlic is crushed completely, again with the flat of the blade. Although both cleaver and board will need to be washed afterwards, this is a lot easier than using a garlic press.

For whole cloves of garlic, or slices, just cut off the root end of the clove and remove the peel with your fingers.

If the garlic is to be used in a spice mix, as is often the case in South-east Asia, put the whole clove in a mortar and give it a blow with a pestle to release the skin. This can then be removed and the garlic crushed with the other ingredients. Recipes indicate whether garlic is to be sliced, chopped or crushed, but as a general rule, crushed garlic is used for overall flavour, the amount determining the intensity. Slices are used for accent, and are sometimes added early in the

cooking process, and then removed once they have imparted a subtle flavour to the dish.

Apart from buying whole cloves of garlic, Asian cooks appreciate the convenience of mInced garlic in jars. Dried garlic is also available, either as granules or flakes. Flakes need to be reconstituted in water before stir-frying, but can be added directly to braised dishes with plenty of liquid. Garlic purée is available in tubes in the West but is not widely used in Asia.

Storage

Look for firm, plump garlic bulbs with clear, papery skins. Avoid any that are beginning to sprout. Garlic bulbs (also called heads) keep well if stored in a cool, dry place. If it is too warm, the cloves will dry out and become powdery.

Making garlic oil

1 Heat 120ml/4fl oz/½ cup oil in a small saucepan. Add 30ml/2 tbsp crushed garlic.

2 Cook gently for about 5 minutes until the garlic is pale gold, stirring occasionally. Do not let it burn or the oil will taste bitter. Cool, strain and use as required.

GINGER

MANDARIN: *JIANG;* CANTONESE: *GEUNG;* THAI: *KHING;* JAPANESE: *SHOGA*

Ginger is believed to be indigenous to the tropical jungles of South-east Asia, and was introduced into China by way of India more than two thousand years ago. The portion of the plant popularly called root ginger is actually a rhizome or underground stem. The colour ranges from pale pink (when very young) to a golden beige, with a dry, papery skin. Ginger is highly valued throughout Asia, not only as an aromatic, but also for its medicinal properties. It is believed to aid digestion, check coughs and quell nausea.

Aroma and flavour

Fresh root ginger (green ginger) has a refreshing scent, reminiscent of citrus, and a pleasant, sharp flavour. Young ginger is tender and mild enough to be stir-fried as a vegetable, while older roots become fibrous and more pungent. Root ginger is available dried, but tastes quite different from fresh. It is used mainly as a pickling spice and Asian cooks would not consider it an acceptable substitute for the fresh root. Ground ginger tastes different again; in Asia its use is limited to mixing with other ground spices such as when making curry powder.

Culinary uses

Root ginger is an indispensable ingredient in Eastern cooking. In China, it is usually paired with spring onions to create a harmonious yin-yang balance in a wide variety of dishes; the cool spring onion providing the yin and the hot ginger the yang. Together they complement (and sometimes tame) the dominant flavours of certain meats and

Above: Fresh root ginger, ground ginger and bottled ginger paste

seafood. Ginger is also used on its own to cut the oily flavour of some cooking oils and marinades. In Thailand, sticks of young ginger are often served as dippers with a spicy sauce, while Indonesians make a wonderful sambal by grinding chillies, shallots and garlic with ginger, and stirring in sugar, salt and rice vinegar. Pickled ginger also plays an important role in oriental cooking. It can be served solo as a side dish, or combined with other ingredients such as beef or duck. One of the most popular items on a Chinese restaurant menu is duck with pineapple and pickled ginger. Chinese pickled ginger is packed in sweetened rice vinegar, and is quite hot. Japanese pickled ginger has a more delicate flavour. The pale pink type called gari is always served with sushi or sashimi to refresh the palate between mouthfuls.

Preparation and cooking techniques

Root ginger is usually peeled before being used. The thin, tough skin is quite easy to scrape or cut away, and the flesh is then thinly sliced, grated, shredded or finely chopped. When the ginger is intended purely for use as a flavouring, and is discarded after cooking, it should be bruised using the flat blade of a knife or cleaver.

Storage

It used to be difficult to get really fresh, juicy root ginger in the shops, but it is now readily available. Look for firm pieces with smooth skin. If bought really fresh, root ginger will keep well for up to two weeks in a cool, dry place, away from strong light. Root ginger can also be frozen. It can be grated straight from the freezer and will thaw on contact with hot food.

Below: Japanese pink, pickled ginger is also known as gari.

Preparing root ginger

1 Thinly peel the skin using a sharp knife or vegetable peeler.

2 Grate the peeled root finely.

3 Alternatively, cut thin slices of ginger into matchstick strips, or coarsely chop the strips.

4 Bruise the root for use in dishes where the ginger will be removed.

GALANGAL

CHINESE: *LIANG JIANG;* THAI: *KHAA;* VIETNAMESE: *CU GIENG*

Like root ginger, galangal is a rhizome that grows underneath the ground. The finger-like protruberances of galangal tend to be thinner and paler in colour, but the two look similar and are used in much the same way. Fresh galangal used to be virtually unobtainable in the West (although it was widely used in medieval Europe), but is now almost as easy to come by as ginger. There are two types. Greater galangal, also known as *lengkuas,* is a native of Indonesia, while lesser galangal originated in southern China. It is not as widely used as its larger relation, but is popular in Thailand, where it is known as *krachai.*

Laos powder is dried galangal that has been ground. Although it does not taste the same as fresh galangal, South-east Asian cooks appreciate its convenience and you will find it in many South-east Asian recipes. As a guide, 5ml/1 tsp of laos powder is equivalent to 1cm/½in fresh galangal, which has been peeled and chopped.

Aroma and flavour

Greater galangal has a pine-like aroma with a correspondingly sharp flavour; lesser galangal is more pungent and the flavour has been likened to a cross between ginger and black pepper. The rhizome is usually used fresh, but is also dried and powdered.

Culinary uses

Galangal is an essential flavouring agent in South-east Asian cooking, particularly in seafood and meat dishes. It is often pounded with shallots, garlic and chillies to make a spice paste for dips or curries. In Thailand, slices of galangal are added to soups, with shreds of lemon grass and lime leaves, while Vietnamese cooks add it to a peanut and lime sauce used to dress meat and vegetable salads.

Preparation and cooking techniques

Fresh galangal should always be peeled. It is usually thinly sliced or cut into matchsticks for cooking. Because it is harder than ginger, you will need to slice it before attempting to crush it, and slices or shreds need to be cooked for somewhat longer than ginger if they are to be tender.

Storage

Fresh galangal will keep for up to 2 weeks if stored in a cool, dry place. It can be stored in the fridge, but it must be well wrapped in greaseproof paper to keep it moist.

Right: Fresh and dried galangal

CHILLIES

MANDARIN: *LAJIAO*; CANTONESE: *LAT JIU*;
THAI: *PRIK*

Chillies are native to tropical
America. Christopher
Columbus introduced
them to Europe,
having come across
them in Mexico while
searching for peppercorns.
Their fame spread rapidly,
and soon they were
being cultivated in
Africa, India and the
Far East, where they rapidly
became an integral part of
the cuisine. There is,
however, a wild variety grown in China's
Sichuan province known as "Towards
Sky Cannon" or "Peacock's Eye Chilli"
(*Capsicum sinense*) which appears to
be native to China. Hot chillies and
sweet peppers belong to the same
genus, capsicum. There are scores of
varieties, but the ones most commonly
used in Asia are the Indian *kalyanpur,
kovilpatt* and *kesanakurru* chillies,
the Japanese *honka* or *hontaka,* the
Korean chilli and the family of Thai
chillies, which includes the fiery bird's
eye. Like sweet peppers, many chillies
start out green and ripen to red, while
others change from yellow to

Below: Green chillies

Below: The same type of chilli can come in various colours.

Right: Red chillies

Chilli paste

Ready-made chilli
paste is sold in
jars, however, it is
easy to make at home.
Simply halve and
seed fresh
chillies, then place them in the
bowl of a food processor and
purée to make a smooth paste.
A chopped onion can be added to
the processor to add bulk to the
paste. Store small amounts of the
paste in the fridge for up to
1 week, or spoon into small
containers, cover and freeze for
up to 6 months. *Sambal oelek*, an
Indonesian chilli sauce, is made
in a similar way, but first the
chillies are blanched.

red and finally to brown or even black,
so what might appear to be a basket of
assorted chillies could turn out to be
the same type of chilli in varying
degrees of ripeness. In size, they range
from tiny pods not much bigger than a
pea to 30cm/12in monsters. Although
Asian cooks tend to use them fresh,
chillies are also available dried.

Aroma and flavour

Although heat is the quality most closely
associated with chillies, flavour is
important too, and aficionados use
terms such as sweet, smoky and
piquant to describe their favourite
types. The degree of heat varies from

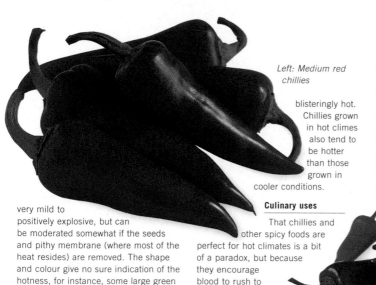

Left: Medium red chillies

blisteringly hot. Chillies grown in hot climes also tend to be hotter than those grown in cooler conditions.

skin, they actually promote cooling. In many Asian countries, they are eaten out of hand, as snacks, and cooks seeking to determine the strength of a chilli before buying will often do so by nibbling a sample from a market stall. Chillies are used fresh, in sauces and salads, and are essential ingredients in Indonesian sambals. They also find their way into a huge variety of cooked dishes, including stocks, soups, braised dishes and stir-fries, either with

very mild to positively explosive, but can be moderated somewhat if the seeds and pithy membrane (where most of the heat resides) are removed. The shape and colour give no sure indication of the hotness, for instance, some large green chillies are very mild, while others are

Culinary uses

That chillies and other spicy foods are perfect for hot climates is a bit of a paradox, but because they encourage blood to rush to the surface of the

Above: Neither the colour nor the size of chillies gives a sure indication of their hotness as some green chillies are hotter than red ones, and some large chillies are hotter than small ones.

Preparing fresh chillies

1 Remove the stalks, then slice the chillies lengthways.

2 Scrape out the pith and seeds from the chillies, then slice, shred or chop the flesh as required. The seeds can be either discarded or added to the dish, depending on the amount of heat that is required.

Preparing dried chillies

1 Remove the stems and seeds and snap each chilli into 2–3 pieces.

2 Put these in a deep bowl, pour over hot water to cover and leave to stand for 30 minutes. Drain, reserving the soaking water if it can usefully be added to the dish, and use the pieces of chilli as they are, or chop them more finely.

or without the seeds. Where just a hint of heat is required, chillies are sometimes added whole to a dish, then removed again just before serving.

Thailand is one of the world's major producers of fresh chillies, so it is not surprising that Thai cooks have developed some of the most exciting and innovative chilli recipes. A favourite way of serving whole chillies is with a pork and prawn stuffing. The chillies are steamed, then fried.

In Chinese cooking, hot chillies are used not to paralyse the tongue but to stimulate the palate. The regional cuisines of Hunan, Jiangxi, Guizhou and Yunnan all feature chillies, although not as strongly as does the province of Sichuan, which is famous for its spicy food. Even in Sichuan, however, chillies are used with discretion and at least a third of Sichuan dishes do not contain any chillies at all. Even the Cantonese use chillies in some of their dishes, and chilli sauce and chilli oil are popular condiments on Cantonese tables.

Making chilli flowers

Thai cooks are famous for their beautiful presentation, and often garnish platters with chilli flowers. These are quite simple to make.

1 Holding each chilli in turn by the stem, slit it in half lengthways.

2 Keeping the stem end of the chilli intact, cut it lengthways into fine strips.

3 Put the prepared chillies in a large bowl of iced water, cover and chill for several hours.

4 The cut chilli strips will curl back to resemble the petals of a flower. Drain well on kitchen paper and use as a garnish. Small chillies may be very hot, so don't be tempted to eat the flowers.

Right: Dried chillies

Using dried chillies

Dry roasting heightens the flavour of dried chillies. Heat a heavy-based frying pan without adding oil. Press the chillies on to the surface of the pan to roast them, but don't allow them to burn, or their flavour will become bitter. Once the chillies are roasted, remove them from the pan and leave to cool, then crush or grind in a mortar with a pestle before adding to dishes.

Preparation and cooking techniques

Chillies must be handled with care. They contain capsaicin, an oily substance which causes intense irritation to sensitive skin. Get capsaicin on your hands, or worse, transfer it to your eyes by rubbing, and you will experience considerable pain. It is therefore very important to wash your hands immediately after handling chillies, and to use plenty of soap, as the oil does not dissolve in water alone. Some cooks prefer to wear latex gloves when preparing chillies, and some become extremely adept at using a knife and fork, and avoid touching the chillies at all, but whichever method you use, remember that it is also essential to wash cutting boards and implements.

Storage

Look for firm, unblemished fruit, avoiding any chillies that are soft or bruised. Some types look wrinkled even in their prime, so do not let this put you off fruit that otherwise appears to be in good condition. The best way to store chillies is to wrap them in kitchen paper, place them in a plastic bag and keep them in the salad compartment of the fridge. They will keep well for a week or more, but it is a good idea to check them occasionally and discard any that begin to show signs of

softening. If you intend to use them solely for cooking, they can be frozen. There is no need to blanch them if you plan to use them fairly quickly. To dry your own chillies, thread them on a string, hang them in a warm place for a week or two until they are dry, then crush them in a mortar with a pestle.

Below: Pickled chillies are available in jars. They are mainly used as a relish.

LEMON GRASS

MANDARIN: *NINGMENG CAO;*
CANTONESE: *XIANG MAO;*
MALAY: *SERAI;* THAI: *TAKRAI;*
VIETNAMESE: *XA*

Few ingredients have seized the Western imagination quite so dramatically as has lemon grass in recent years. At one time this scented grass was little known outside South-east Asia; today it is to be found in nearly every supermarket. Lemon grass is a perennial tufted plant with a bulbous base. It grows in dense clumps in tropical and subtropical countries and is commercially cultivated on a grand scale. The cut stems are about 20cm/8in long, and look a little like fat spring onions or very skinny leeks.

Aroma and flavour

It is only when the stems are cut that the distinctive citrus aroma can be fully appreciated. This is matched by the clean, intense lemon flavour, which has a hint of ginger but none of the acidity associated with lemon or grapefruit.

Below: Dried lemon grass

Left: Lemon grass

Lemon rind is sometimes suggested as a substitute, but it lacks the intensity and liveliness of fresh lemon grass, and will give disappointing results. Ground dried lemon grass, also known as serai powder, can be used instead of fresh. As a guide, about 5ml/1 tsp powder is equivalent to 1 fresh stalk. Whole and dried chopped stalks are also available in jars from oriental stores and larger supermarkets, as are jars of lemon grass paste.

Culinary uses

Lemon grass is widely used throughout South-east Asia, in soups, sauces, stir-fries, curries, salads, pickles and marinades. It is a perfect partner for coconut milk, especially in fish, seafood and chicken dishes. Thai cooks often start a stir-fry by adding a few rings of lemon grass and perhaps a little grated or chopped fresh root ginger or galangal to the oil. This not only flavours the oil, but also fills the room with a glorious aroma. A favourite Vietnamese dish consists of sea bream coated in a lemon grass paste, which is left to stand until the flavour penetrates the fish, and then fried.

Preparation and cooking techniques

There are two main ways of using lemon grass. The stalk can be bruised, then cooked slowly in a soup or stew until it releases all its flavour and is removed, or the tender portions of the lemon grass (usually the lower 5cm/2in of the bulbous end of the stem) can be sliced or finely chopped,

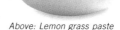

Above: Lemon grass paste

then stir-fried or used in a salad or braised dish. Often one stalk will serve both purposes, the tougher top end is used for background flavouring while the tender portion forms the focal point of a dish. For basting food that is to be grilled or barbecued, the upper portion of the lemon grass stalk can be used. The fibrous end is flattened with a cleaver or pestle to make a brush.

Storage

Store lemon grass stalks in a paper bag in the vegetable compartment of the fridge. They will keep for 2–3 weeks.

Making a lemon grass brush
Instead of discarding the dry stalk, make it into a basting brush.

Trim off the bottom 5cm/2in of the lemon grass stalk to use in a recipe, then flatten the cut end of the remaining stalk using a cleaver or pestle to produce a fibrous brush.

KAFFIR LIMES

THAI: *BAI MAKRUT;* INDONESIAN: *DAUN JERAK;*
VIETNAMESE: *CHANH SAC;* MALAYSIAN: *LIMAU
PURUT;* BURMESE: *SHAUK-NU*

These fruit are not true limes, but
belong to a subspecies of the citrus
family. Native to South-east Asia, they
have dark green knobbly skins, quite
unlike those of their cousins, the
smooth-skinned limes or lemons. The
fruit is not edible. The rind is
sometimes used in cooking, but it is the
leaves that are most highly prized. Kaffir
limes yield very little juice, and what
there is is very sour. Thai and Malaysian
cooks occasionally use it to heighten
the flavour of dishes with a citrus base.
Vietnamese women use the juice as a
hair rinse.

Japanese citron peel

In Japan, very thin slices of
citron peel *(yuzu)* are used
to garnish soups. The
ground peel is used to
flavour miso.

Aroma and flavour

The scented bouquet
is unmistakably
citrus, and the full
lemon flavour is
released when the
leaves are torn
or shredded.

Culinary uses

Kaffir lime leaves are
synonymous with Thai cooking,
and are also used in Indonesia,
Malaysia, Burma and Vietnam. The
leaves are torn or finely shredded
and used in soups (especially hot and
sour soups) and curries. The
finely grated rind
is sometimes
added to fish or
chicken dishes.

Storage

Fresh kaffir limes and leaves are
obtainable in oriental stores. They will
keep for several days, or can be frozen.
Freeze-dried kaffir lime leaves are also
available. These are used in much the
same way as bay leaves, and do not
need to be soaked in water first.
Stored in a sealed container in a
cool, dry place, the dried leaves
will keep their flavour for only
a few months.

ORANGE OR TANGERINE PEEL

MANDARIN: *CHEN PI;*
CANTONESE: *CHAN PEI*

Both oranges and tangerines
originated in China, where they
were held in high regard for
centuries before traders
introduced them to the
West. The sun-dried
peel of both these
citrus fruits is
used as a spice,
particularly in
the cooking
of Sichuan
and Hunan.

Left: Dried orange peel

*Above: Kaffir
limes and kaffir
lime leaves*

Aroma and flavour

The dried peel is dark brown and brittle,
but retains a strong citrus fragrance.
When it is used in cooking, it imparts a
tangy flavour to the food.

Culinary uses

Originally, dried citrus peels were mainly
used medicinally. Today, they are a
popular seasoning and are often
combined with star anise and cinnamon
when braising meat or poultry.

Preparation and cooking techniques

In braised dishes, pieces of dried peel
are used in much the same way as star
anise, and are discarded after cooking.
When peel is used in a stir-fry, however,
it is first soaked in water until soft, and
the pith is scraped off before the peel is
shredded or sliced.

Storage

Orange and tangerine peel are sold in
plastic bags in oriental stores. Once
opened, the bags should be resealed
and kept in a cool, dry, dark place. The
peel will keep for many months.

CURRY LEAVES

INDONESIAN: *DAUN KARI*; THAI: *BAI KAREE*;
BURMESE: *PINDOSIN*

These are the shiny green leaves of a hardwood tree that is indigenous to India. They are widely used in Indian cooking, especially in South India and Sri Lanka, and were introduced into Malaysia by Tamil immigrants. The spear-shaped leaves grow on a thin stem. They are slightly serrated, with a pale underside, and are not unlike small bay leaves.

Aroma and flavour

Curry leaves have an intriguing warm fragrance, with just a hint of sweet, green pepper or tangerine. The full flavour is released when the leaves are bruised. When added to curries or braised dishes, they impart a distinctive flavour. Dried curry leaves come a very poor second to fresh, and rapidly lose their fragrance.

Culinary uses

The leaves are used whole or torn in Indian, Malay and Indonesian curries. Fried in ghee, with mustard seeds, they make a good addition to dhals.

Preparation and cooking techniques

Rinse the leaves and then strip from the stems. Use the leaves whole or chopped as directed in recipes.

Left: Dried curry leaves

Storage

Fresh curry leaves can be bought from shops selling Indian and Gujerati produce. They will keep for several days in the fridge, but should be closely wrapped to prevent their distinctive flavour from being transferred to other items. Alternatively – and this is more convenient – open freeze the leaves, then transfer them to a plastic box. Dried leaves do not have much taste, unless you can locate the vacuum-packed variety, which have better colour and flavour.

MINT

CHINESE: *PAK HOM HO*; INDONESIAN: *DAUN PUDINA*; THAI: *BAI SARANAI*; VIETNAMESE: *HUNG QUE*

Mint originated in the Mediterranean region, but it spread rapidly throughout the world. There are many types grown in Asia, but the most commonly used is a tropical variety of spearmint, which has grey-green oval leaves.

Aroma and flavour

Mint has a fresh, stimulating aroma. The Asian variety is much more strongly flavoured than most European types, and is slightly sweet tasting, imparting a cool aftertaste.

Culinary uses

Mint is an essential ingredient in Vietnamese cooking, and it was they who introduced it to the Thais. Its fresh flavour is enjoyed in many salads, and in the delicious rice paper rolls that go by the name of *goi cuon*. Thai cooks like to add a handful of mint leaves just before serving some of their soups and highly spiced dishes. As it has such a dominant flavour, mint is seldom used with other herbs.

Preparation

Wash the leaves on the stem under cold water, shake off the excess moisture and pat dry using kitchen paper.

Storage

Wrap loosely in kitchen paper and keep in the vegetable compartment of the fridge, or stand the stems in a jug of cold water covered with a plastic bag and keep in the door of the fridge.

Below: Mint

BASIL

THAI: *BAI HORAPA* (SWEET BASIL), *BAI
KRAPOW* (HOLY BASIL), *BAI MANGLAK* (HAIRY
OR LEMON-SCENTED BASIL); INDONESIAN:
INDRING; JAPANESE: *MEBOKI*

Basil is one of the oldest
herbs known to man. It is
an annual and is believed
to have originated in
India. Hindus hold it
sacred and often
plant it around
their holy places.
In India, however, it is not used in
cooking as much as it is in the rest of
Asia. In Vietnam, Laos and Cambodia it
is an important ingredient, but it is in
Thailand that basil is most widely used,
and it is the varieties of basil favoured
by the Thais that you
will find most
frequently in oriental
shops in the West.
Horapa (sweet
basil) comes
closest to the
Mediterranean
varieties with which we
are most familiar. It
has shiny green
leaves and the stems
are sometimes purple. *Krapow,*
commonly known as holy basil, is
another sweet basil, but with narrower
leaves that tend to be dull rather than
shiny. The leaves have serrated red or
purple edges. Thais also use a lemon-
scented basil – sometimes called hairy
basil – but this does not travel well and
is seldom seen outside Thailand. If you
cannot obtain Asian basil when cooking
an oriental dish, any European variety
can be used instead, but the flavour
will not be the same, and you should
use a little more than the amount
recommended. Basil is best used fresh,
but freeze-dried leaves are also
available from larger supermarkets.

Aroma and flavour

Of the Asian basils, *horapa* has a faint
aniseed flavour, while holy basil is more
pungent. Hairy basil has a lemon scent
and is slightly peppery.

*Above: Sweet
basil*

Below: Thai basil

Culinary uses

Sweet basil leaves are added to curries
or salads both as an ingredient and also
as a garnish. They impart a fresh spicy
flavour. Holy basil leaves only release
their full flavour when cooked and are
therefore frequently used in stir-fries.

Preparation

Strip the leaves from the stem and
either tear them into pieces or add
them whole to the other ingredients.
Avoid chopping basil leaves.

Storage

Wrap
bunches of
basil loosely
in kitchen
paper and keep
them in the salad
compartment of the
fridge. Alternatively, stand

Growing basil

If you have difficulty
locating supplies of fresh
basil for Thai or Vietnamese
recipes, it might be worth growing
your own from seed. Many garden
centres and hardware stores sell
the full range of Asian varieties,
and they do well wherever the
climate is relatively mild. Start
them off in pots on a warm
window sill, and move them to a
sunny patio after the threat of
frost has passed.

the stems in a jug of water covered with
a plastic bag. Keep them in the fridge
and change the water every day.

SHISO

JAPANESE: *SHISO* (GREEN),
AKA SHISO (RED); KOREAN:
KKAENNIP

Also known as *perilla* or the
beefsteak plant, this annual herb is
grown in China, Korea, Laos and
Vietnam and is very well known in
Japan, where it is also called *oba.* The
leaves can be green or reddish-purple.
When crushed, they release a pungent
aroma, similar to that of mint. Japanese
cooks use shiso in tempura and when
making *umeboshi* (pickled plums).
In the presence of an acid, the
red-leafed variety dyes
ginger red.

Above: Shiso

CORIANDER

MANDARIN: *XIANGCAI;* CANTONESE: *YUAN SUI;*
BURMESE: *NAN NAN BIN;* THAI: *PAK CHEE*

Also known as Chinese parsley – and
familiar to Americans as cilantro –
coriander is one of the oldest known
herbs in the world, and also one of
the most popular. Although a native
of southern Europe, fresh coriander
has become an indispensable
ingredient throughout Asia and
the Middle East, as well as
in Latin America.

*Above: Coriander –
Asian cooks use the
roots as well as the leaves
and stems.*

Below: Ground coriander

Aroma and flavour

Coriander takes its name from
the Greek *koris,* meaning a bug. The
leaves of the plant are supposed to give
off a smell similar to that of a room
infested with bed bugs, yet the Chinese,
displaying a wicked sense of humour,
call coriander "fragrant leaves". When
dry-fried, the seeds smell rather like
burnt orange, while the ground seeds
impart a warm, spicy aroma to food.

Culinary uses

Asian cooks use every part of the plant:
the stems are used for flavouring; the
leaves in stir-fries, soups and noodle
dishes; and as a garnish, the seeds for
spice pastes and
in curries. Ground
coriander is widely used, often in
combination with ground cumin.
In Thailand, the roots are
used, too. This can
present problems for
the Western cook,
because the thin roots
are usually removed
before the coriander
reaches the market. One
answer is to grow your
own, but if this is
impractical, use the bottom
portion of the stem as
a substitute.

Preparation and cooking techniques

Try not to chop fresh
coriander too finely, or
the beauty of the
serrated leaves will be
lost. Never overcook
the leaves or they will
become limp and
unpalatable; either
use them raw as a
garnish, or add them
to a dish at the very
last moment.
  If a recipe
calls for ground
coriander, it is

Left: Coriander seeds

preferable to dry-fry and grind the
seeds yourself, as the aroma and
flavour will be more pronounced than
when ready-ground coriander is used.

Storage

Fresh coriander will not keep for more
than a couple of days unless stood in a
jug of cold water and covered with a
plastic bag, in which case it will stay
fresh for a little longer. Coriander roots
are seldom available, but if you do
locate a supply, the cleaned roots can
be frozen.
  Dried coriander seeds keep well, but
the ready-ground powder rapidly loses
its aroma and flavour. Buy small
quantities so that you can replenish
your supplies regularly.

Right:
Ground
and fresh
turmeric

TURMERIC

BURMESE: *HSANWEN;* MANDARIN: *WONG GEUNG;* CANTONESE: *YU CHIN;* JAPANESE: *UKON*

Turmeric comes from the ginger family but does not have the characteristic "heat" associated with fresh ginger. The plant, a rhizome, is indigenous to hot, humid, hilly areas of South-east Asia from Vietnam to Southern India. Frequently referred to as "Indian saffron", it shares with saffron the capacity to tint foods yellow, but is nowhere near as subtle as the much more expensive spice. The bright yellow colour, which can clearly be seen when the rhizome is sliced, is also used as a dye of silks and cottons, including the fabric used to make robes for Buddhist monks. When mixed to a paste, turmeric is sometimes smeared on the cheeks to protect the skin from the sun. The world's largest producer of turmeric is India, but Indonesia and China also grow significant quantities of this spice.

The bulk of the turmeric crop is used for domestic consumption or ground and sold as powder.

Aroma and flavour

Fresh turmeric is sometimes available from oriental stores. When cut it has a peppery aroma with a hint of wood in the background. It imparts a warm, slightly musky flavour and a rich colour to any food with which it is cooked. The dried spice has similar properties.

Culinary uses

Ground turmeric is an essential ingredient in curry powders, being responsible for the characteristic yellow colour. It is also used in the preparation of some blends of mustard powder and is the spice that gives piccalilli its lurid colour. That famous Anglo-Indian breakfast dish – kedgeree – contains turmeric, and it is also used in pilau rice, dhals and vegetable dishes. Turmeric has a natural affinity with fish, and is often used in Malayan recipes.

Preparation and cooking methods

Using a sharp knife, slice off the skin, then slice, grate or chop the flesh. It can be ground with other ingredients to make a curry paste. Some people like to wear gloves when preparing fresh turmeric as it can stain the skin. Ground dried turmeric is easy to use as it needs no preparation.

Storage

Fresh turmeric will keep for up to 2 weeks, if stored in a cool, dry place away from strong light. It can be stored in the fridge, but must be well wrapped to keep it moist. Like all ground spices, ground turmeric will lose its potency on keeping, so buy only small quantities and keep the powder in an airtight container in a cupboard away from strong light. The only time whole pieces of dried turmeric are likely to be called for is in the preparation of some pickles. Do not attempt to grind the whole dried spice to make powder; the rhizomes are too hard.

Preparing fresh turmeric

1 Using a sharp knife, scrape off the skin.

2 Grate the flesh using a standard box grater, or slice or chop, depending on the recipe.

*Above: Star-shaped
star anise*

STAR ANISE

MANDARIN: *PAK KOK;* CANTONESE: *BOAT GOK;*
INDONESIAN: *BUNGA LAWANG;* THAI: *POY
KAK BUA*

Star anise is the unusual star-shaped
fruit of an evergreen tree native to
South-west China and Vietnam. The
tree has yellow flowers that resemble
narcissus. These give way to the star-
like fruits, which are harvested before
they ripen. The points of the star
contain amber seeds. Both the seeds
and the husk are used for the ground
spice. In China, one point, the name
given to one section of the star, is often
chewed after a meal as a digestive.

Aroma and flavour

Star anise both smells and tastes like
liquorice. The flavour can also be
detected in the alcoholic drinks pastis
and anisette.

Culinary uses

The aromatic flavour of star anise
complements rich meats. Star
anise is very popular in Chinese
cuisine, especially with pork and
duck, and it is used to flavour
beef soups in Vietnam. It is also
sometimes used in sweet
dishes, such as fruit salads.
Ground star anise is one of the
main ingredients of five spice powder.

Preparation and cooking methods

Star anise can be added whole, and
looks so attractive that it is often left in
a dish when serving, even though it no
longer fulfils any culinary function.
When a small quantity is required, the
spice can be broken and just one or two
points or segments added. It is possible
to grind star anise at home, but it
should be used sparingly as it has a
quite powerful flavour.

Storage

As a whole spice star anise has a long
shelf life. Buy the ground spice in small
quantities from a shop with a high
turnover of stock, and store in a cool,
dry place, away from direct light, to
retain the maximum aroma and flavour.

*Below: The best cloves are plump
and unbroken.*

CLOVES

MANDARIN: *TING HSIANG;* CANTONESE;
DING HEUNG; JAPANESE: *CHOJI;*
THAI: *KAAN PLOO*

Cloves are the unopened
flower buds of a tree which is
a member of the myrtle family.
They originated in the Spice
Islands in Indonesia and were taken
to the Seychelles and Mauritius early
in the 18th century. The biggest
producer now is Zanzibar where the
fresh pink buds are picked twice a year.
They are then dried on palm leaf mats
or over a gentle heat when they turn the
familiar reddish brown. The name clove
is derived from the Latin *clavus,*
meaning a nail.

Aroma and flavour

Cloves have an intense fragrance and
an aromatic flavour that can be fiery.
They are slightly astringent.

Culinary uses

In Asia, cloves are mainly used in
savoury dishes, and their warm
aromatic flavour complements rich
meats. Thai cooks use cloves to cut the
rich flavour of duck, and also use them
with tomatoes, salty vegetables and in
ham or pork dishes. Ground cloves are
an essential ingredient in many spice
mixtures, including the famous Chinese
five spice powder. They are also one of
the ingredients in Worcestershire sauce.

Preparation

Cloves need no preparation. When
purchasing, look for plump cloves.

Storage

Whole cloves have a long shelf life if
kept in a cool place. Ground cloves
should be bought in small
quantities and stored in an
airtight jar away from
strong light, so that the
spice retains its colour and
flavour. To make a small
amount of ground cloves,
crush the central bud at
the top of the clove and
use immediately.

Above: Cinnamon sticks and ground cinnamon

CINNAMON

INDONESIAN: *KAYU MANIS PADANG;* THAI: *OB CHUEY*

The best quality cinnamon is grown in Sri Lanka but it also flourishes elsewhere in Asia, particularly on the coastal strip of South India and Burma. The spice is actually the bark of a bushy tree that is a member of the laurel family. After three years, the branches are cut off and a long incision is made in the bark, so that this can be lifted off. The operation is carried out during the rainy season, when the humidity speeds the peeling process. The bark is then dried in the sun and hand rolled to produce the familiar quills or sticks. Ground cinnamon is also produced.

Aroma and flavour

Cinnamon has a delightfully exotic bouquet, sweet and fragrant, thanks to an essential oil, oil of cinnamon, which is used medicinally. The flavour is warm and aromatic.

Culinary uses

Cinnamon has universal appeal as a flavouring both in sweet and savoury dishes and in a multitude of cakes and breads. In Asia, the sticks are used in spicy meat dishes, often with star anise, with which cinnamon has an affinity. Indonesian cooks use cinnamon in their famous spiced beef and coconut milk stew known as rendang.

Preparation

Add the whole or broken cinnamon stick as directed in the recipe. The sticks are very hard and it is difficult to grind them at home, so it is preferable to buy ready-ground cinnamon.

Storage

Cinnamon sticks have a long shelf life, and will keep for a year or more in an airtight container. Buy ground cinnamon in small quantities from a shop with a high turnover of stock and store it in an airtight container away from both heat and strong light.

Below: Ground cassia and cassia bark

CASSIA

CHINESE: *KUEI;* JAPANESE: *KEIHI;* THAI: *OB CHOEY*

Cassia is sometimes known as Chinese cinnamon. Like cinnamon, it comes from the bark of a tree which is related to laurel, but whereas cinnamon is native to Sri Lanka, cassia comes from Burma, and is also cultivated in China, Indo-China and Indonesia. It is harvested in much the same way as cinnamon, but the bark is not as fine, so although it curls, it will not form the fine quills we associate with cinnamon.

Aroma and flavour

Cassia smells rather like cinnamon, but is more pungent.

Culinary uses

Chinese cooks make much use of cassia. It is one of the constituents of five spice powder and is also an important ingredient in the elaborate spiced stock known as *lu* which is used throughout China for simmering foods. When this stock is first made, it is very strongly flavoured, and is generally used for cooking beef, pot-roast style. The stock is not served with the beef, but is saved to be used again, perhaps with poultry. It may well be boiled up a third time, to simmer

fish or shellfish. In some homes, a pan of *lu* will be kept going for months. Cracked cassia quills and cassia buds (which look like cloves) are used in the East to give a warm aromatic flavour to pickles, curries and spiced meat dishes.

Preparation and cooking methods

Cassia is quite tough. Break the pieces as required with the end of a rolling pin or put them in a mortar and use a stout pestle to shatter them. Where ground cassia is required, it is best to buy it in that form.

Storage

As for cinnamon.

CUMIN

CHINESE: *KUMING;* JAPANESE: *KUMIN;* THAI: *YEERAA*

Cumin has been cultivated since earliest times. It is believed to have originated in the Eastern Mediterranean, but is now widely cultivated, especially in China, India, Indonesia and Japan. The plant is a member of the parsley family, but only the seeds (whole or ground) are used in cooking.

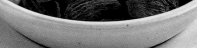

Above: Small green and large black cardamom pods

Aroma and flavour

Cumin has a sweet spicy aroma and the flavour is pungent and slightly bitter.

Culinary uses

Cumin is often partnered with whole or ground coriander seeds. Indian cooks are particularly partial to cumin, and it was they who introduced the spice to Singapore, Malaysia and Indonesia.

Preparation

To bring out their full flavour, the seeds are often dry-fried. They are then used whole or ground in a spice mill or in a mortar using a pestle.

Storage

Buy the whole spice in small quantities. Store in a cool place away from bright light. For best results dry-fry and grind the whole spice as

and when required. You can buy ready ground cumin from supermarkets, but it loses its flavour rapidly.

CARDAMOM

BURMESE: *PHALAZEE;* JAPANESE: *KARUDAMON;* THAI: *LUK KRAVAN*

A native of South India, cardamom is a tall herbaceous perennial belonging to the ginger family. It is largely grown for its pods, although Thai cooks sometimes use the leaves for flavouring. The pods are either added whole to spicy dishes, or opened so that the tiny dark seeds can be extracted. The most familiar pods are pale green, and there are also white pods, which are simply bleached green ones. Black cardamoms, which come from Vietnam and India, are large and coarse, and taste quite different. Cardamom pods are harvested by hand, and this makes them more costly than most other spices.

Aroma and flavour

Cardamoms are sweet, pungent and highly aromatic. They have a pleasantly warm flavour, with hints of lemon and eucalyptus. When chewed after a meal, the pods are said to aid digestion as well as sweeten the breath.

Culinary uses

Indian cooks use cardamom to flavour curries, pilaus and desserts, so it is not surprising that the spice is popular wherever there are Indian communities.

Preparation

The pods can be used whole or bruised and dry-fried to enhance the flavour. If just the seeds are required, discard the outer husks. For ground cardamom, grind the seeds in a mortar using a pestle.

Storage

Buy the whole pods and store in an airtight jar in a cool dry place. Grind seeds as required.

Above: Cumin seeds and ground cumin

FENNEL SEEDS

MANDARIN: *WOOI HEUNG;* CANTONESE: *HUI XIANG;* THAI: *YIRA*

Although native to the Mediterranean, this member of the parsley family is widely grown in India and Japan. The ridged seeds are sage green in colour.

Aroma and flavour

Sweet, warm and aromatic, fennel seeds have a distinct anise flavour.

Culinary uses

Fennel seeds are a constituent in many spice mixtures, especially those that are intended to be used with fish or shellfish. Ground fennel is one of the constituents of Chinese five spice powder.

Preparation

Dry-fry before grinding to release the full flavour of the spice.

Storage

Buy small quantities of seeds at a time and store in an airtight jar away from strong light.

Above: Fennel seeds

Chinese five spice powder

Close your eyes as you enter a Chinese supermarket or store and the distinctive aroma of Chinese five spice power seems to dominate. This reddish brown spice mixture is classically composed of equal quantities of Sichuan peppercorns, cassia or cinnamon, cloves, fennel seeds and star anise. Blends vary, however, and ginger, galangal, black cardamom and liquorice can be included. Ginger gives the spice blend a sweeter flavour, and this version is used in desserts. Five spice powder is very popular in China, and is particularly complementary when used with duck, pork, red cooked meats (cooked in soy sauce) and barbecued meats such as spare ribs. Make your own powder by grinding equal amounts of the five spices with a mortar and pestle, or buy the ready ground powder in small quantities and store in an airtight jar away from strong light. A five spice paste is now available in small jars from many of the larger supermarkets.

Japanese seven spice powder

Seven spice powder, which is also known as *shichimi-togarashi,* seven flavour seasoning or seven taste powder, is a delicious condiment that the Japanese like to shake on to food at the table much as we would use salt and pepper. It is especially popular as a seasoning for soups and noodles and other dishes such as sukiyaki and tempura. *Shichimi* is made from a combination of the following ingredients: ground chilli, hemp seed, poppy seed, rape seed, *sansho* (the Japanese name for Sichuan pepper-corns), black and

Right: Chinese five spice powder (top) and Japanese seven spice powder (bottom) can be bought ready-ground from supermarkets and Asian stores.

white sesame seeds, and dried ground tangerine peel. In some mixes ground nori (seaweed) is added. It would be usual to buy this mixture ready prepared. Blends of this spice mixture vary, from mild to very sharp.

PEPPER

MANDARIN: *HU-CHIAO;* CANTONESE: *WOO JIU;*
INDONESIAN: *MERICA;* THAI: *PRIK THAI;*
VIETNAMESE: *HAT-TRIEU*

Often referred to as the king of spices,
pepper has an ancient and illustrious
past. Known and valued in India for
over two thousand years, it was
introduced into Europe in the 4th
century BC. Demand rapidly grew, but
transporting the spice across Asia by
the caravan routes was costly, and the
monopoly meant that the prices
remained astronomically high. Even in
Roman times there was outrage that the
spices were sold at one hundred times
their original cost.

It was the demand for pepper that
inspired the search for sailing routes to
the East which changed the course of
history. When the Portuguese explorer
Vasco da Gama opened up the sea
route to India in the 15th century,
Lisbon became the spice capital of the
world, but still the prices stayed high.
Even today pepper is the most
important spice on world markets, both
in terms of value and volume.

Pepper is a perennial climbing vine
indigenous to the Malabar coast of India
where it is said that the best pepper is
still produced. It grows best near the
equator and is cultivated intensively
in Sarawak and Thailand, as well as in
tropical Africa and Brazil. In the
Malayan state of Sarawak the vines are
trained up long ironwood frames or
round tree trunks. The vines have
to be controlled

Green peppercorns

These are simply
unripe berries. They
are sold on the stem in
some Thai supermarkets, and
are a popular ingredient in that
country. They can be used fresh,
but are also dried, pickled or
canned. Those that are bottled
or canned need to be rinsed and
drained, then added whole or
crushed as the recipe dictates.
Freeze-dried green peppercorns
can be ground in a peppermill.
Green peppercorns have a less
complex flavour than white or
black peppercorns but are still
quite fiery.

*Above: Fresh green
peppercorns are sometimes
sold on the stem in Thai
supermarkets.*

to prevent them from climbing too high,
which would make harvesting difficult.
The leaves are long, green and pointed,
and white flowers blossom on the
catkins or "spikes".

The plant starts fruiting three to five
years after planting, and the harvest
continues every three years thereafter
for forty years, which is the life of the
plant. When the berries are harvested
they are still unripe and green. In
Sarawak they are dried on mats in the
sun, and are raked frequently until the
skin shrivels and the berries darken to
become the familiar black peppercorns.
Another method is to immerse the
berries in boiling water, drain them well,
and then dry them in kilns.

White peppercorns are
husked ripe
berries. The
berries are
picked
when
they are
red or
orange.
They are
soaked in
running water
for several
days, and then they
are trampled underfoot
to loosen the husks. Finally the

pepper berries are transferred to
rattan baskets, where they are washed
and the husks and stalks removed by
hand to leave the white peppercorns.
These are then left to dry on mats in the
sun for several weeks, or kiln-dried.

Aroma and flavour

Black peppercorns have an earthy
aroma, which is particularly noticeable
when they are crushed. The flavour is
hot and pungent. White peppercorns
are slightly milder.

Culinary uses

Pepper is the one spice which is used
before, during and after cooking. Its
value as a seasoning is legendary, for it
not only has its own flavour, but has the
ability to enhance the flavour of other
ingredients in a dish.

Preparation

Use a peppermill and grind fresh
black pepper as it is required. White
peppercorns are less pungent and are
used where flecks of black might spoil
the appearance of a dish, such as a
light-coloured sauce.

Storage

Buy whole peppercorns. Store in a cool
place in an airtight container. They keep
for a long time.

*Right:
Black and
white peppercorns*

SICHUAN/SZECHUAN PEPPER

MANDARIN: *FAA JIU;* CANTONESE: *HU CHIAO;*
JAPANESE: *SANSHO*

To call this "pepper" is misleading. This spice actually comes from the prickly ash tree, which is native to the Sichuan province in China, but also grows elsewhere in Asia. Unusually, it is the seed pods themselves, not the seeds they contain, that are used for the spice. The tiny reddish brown pods or husks are harvested when ripe, the bitter black seeds are removed and discarded, and the pods – Sichuan peppercorns – are either added whole to stewed dishes or dried and ground as a seasoning spice.

The prickly ash also grows in Japan, where the ripened pods are called *mizansho* or Japanese peppercorns. When ground, the spice is known as *konazansho* or *sansho.* The wood of the prickly ash is sometimes used to make mortar and pestle sets, which are much sought after by Japanese cooks who claim they impart a subtle flavour when used to grind ingredients.

Left: Sichuan peppercorns

Aroma and flavour

Not as pungent as true pepper, Sichuan peppercorns have a warm aroma with a hint of citrus. The full flavour is released when they are dry-fried.

Culinary uses

Sichuan peppercorns are immensely popular in Chinese cuisine. They are excellent in duck, pork and chicken dishes. The ground peppercorns are used in both Chinese five spice powder and Japanese seven spice powder.

Preparation

The dried seed pods should be picked over carefully to remove any debris. Dry-fry the seed pods to heighten their flavour, then use as directed in recipes.

Storage

Although it is possible to buy ground Sichuan pepper, it is better to buy the peppercorns whole and grind them after dry-frying. Keep them in an airtight jar.

Wasabi

Sometimes described as horseradish mustard, this has much in common with both, although it is related to neither. Wasabi is a Japanese seasoning, derived from a slow-growing plant that is found near mountain streams. The peeled root reveals vivid green flesh. This is very finely grated, preferably on sharkskin, and then dried or powdered. When mixed to a cream with soy sauce or water, it makes an extremely hot condiment, which is traditionally served with sushi and sashimi.

Above: A tube of ready-made apple-green wasabi paste

Right: Wasabi powder is mixed to a paste with a little water or soy sauce

MUSTARD

MALAY: *BIJI SAVI*

Mustard is one of the oldest spices known to man and has been cultivated as a crop for thousands of years. Both white *(alba)* and black *(nigra)* mustard seeds are indigenous to the Mediterranean region, while brown mustard seeds *(juncea)* are native to India. The word mustard

Below: Brown, black and white mustard seeds

Dry-frying mustard seeds

Mustard seeds have almost no smell until they are heated, so before adding them to dishes, they should be dry-fried to heighten their aroma.

1 Heat a little sunflower oil in a deep, wide pan. Add the seeds and shake the pan over the heat, stirring occasionally, until they start to change colour.

2 Have a pan lid ready to prevent the mustard seeds from popping out of the pan.

comes from the Latin *mustum* or *must*, the newly pressed grape juice that Romans mixed with the ground seeds to make what was aptly described as *mustum ardens* (the burning paste).

In Asia, the mustard plant is valued as much for its dark green leaves, which are called mustard greens and are a popular vegetable, as for its seeds. Mustard powders and pastes are not as widely used as they are in Europe or America.

Aroma and flavour

Mustard seeds have no aroma in their raw state. When they are roasted, however, they develop a rich, nutty small. Mustard's famous hot taste comes from an enzyme in the seeds, which is only activated when they are crushed and mixed with warm water. Brown mustard seeds, which have largely replaced the black seeds, are not as intensely pungent. White mustard seeds, which are actually a pale honey colour, are slightly larger than the other two varieties and a little milder.

Culinary uses

Throughout Asia, mustard seeds are used for pickling and seasoning. The whole seeds are often used in vegetable and dhal dishes, especially in countries such as Malaysia.

Preparation and cooking techniques

Mustard seeds are frequently roasted or fried before being used to bring out their flavour. A southern Indian technique involves spooning the seeds into hot ghee or oil, with a few curry leaves for extra flavour. A lid is placed over the pan to contain the seeds, which soon begin to splutter and pop. The seeds and oil are then poured, still sizzling, on to hot vegetable dishes, soups, stews or dhal as a flavoursome topping. Mustard oil is occasionally used for frying the seeds.

Mustard powder is used as a condiment. When it is mixed with warm water, milk or beer, a chemical reaction begins which allows the mustard to achieve its maximum potency. It takes about 15 minutes for the full flavour to develop. Boiling water or vinegar would inhibit the action of the enzyme responsible for the process, so should not be used.

Storage

Mustard seeds keep well. Store them in an airtight jar in a cool place.

Left: Tamarind block

may suggest using vinegar or lemon juice instead, but the results will not compare with using the real thing.

Preparation

Compressed tamarind This comes in a solid block and looks rather like a packet of dried dates. To prepare it, tear off a piece that is roughly equivalent to 15ml/1 tbsp and soak it in 150ml/¼ pint/⅔ cup warm water for about 10 minutes. Swirl the tamarind around with your fingers so that the pulp is released from the seeds. Using a nylon sieve, strain the juice into a jug. Discard the contents of the sieve and use the

TAMARIND

CHINESE: *ASAM KOH;* INDONESIAN: *ASAM JAVA;* THAI: *MAK KHAM;* BURMESE: *MA-GYI-THI*

The handsome tamarind tree, commonly called the "date of India", is believed to be a native of East Africa but is now cultivated in India, South-east Asia and the West Indies. The brown fruit pods are 15–20cm/6–8in long. Inside, the seeds are surrounded by a sticky brown pulp. This does not look very prepossessing, but is one of the treasures of the East. It has a high tartaric acid content, and is widely used as a souring agent.

dried tamarind have been around for a while, but it is now also possible to buy jars of fresh tamarind and cartons of tamarind concentrate and paste. There is no substitute for tamarind. Some recipes

Aroma and flavour

Tamarind doesn't have much of an aroma, but the flavour is wonderful. It is tart and sour without being bitter, and fruity and refreshing.

Culinary uses

Tamarind is used in many curries, chutneys and dhals, and is an essential ingredient of Thai hot and sour soups. It is also one of the ingredients in Worcestershire sauce. Tamarind is available in a variety of forms. Blocks of compressed tamarind and slices of

Above, from top: Tamarind paste, tamarind pods and dried tamarind slices

Stir-fried Prawns with Tamarind

Tamarind is used in many Thai dishes to give them a characteristic sour, tangy flavour. Fresh tamarind pods from the tamarind tree can sometimes be bought, but preparing them for cooking is a laborious process. The Thais usually prefer to use compressed blocks of tamarind paste, which is simply soaked in warm water and then strained.

SERVES 4–6

50g/2oz compressed tamarind
150ml/¼ pint/⅔ cup boiling
  water
30ml/2 tbsp vegetable oil
30ml/2 tbsp chopped onion
30ml/2 tbsp palm sugar
30ml/2 tbsp chicken stock
15ml/1 tbsp fish sauce
6 dried red chillies, fried
450g/1lb raw shelled prawns
15ml/1 tbsp fried chopped garlic
30ml/2 tbsp fried sliced shallots
chopped and shredded spring
  onions, to garnish

1 Put the tamarind in a bowl, pour over the boiling water and stir well to break up any lumps. Leave for 10 minutes. Meanwhile, heat the oil in a wok. Add the chopped onion and stir-fry until golden brown.

2 Strain the tamarind juice, pushing as much of the juice through as possible. Measure 90ml/6 tbsp of the juice. Add to the wok along with the sugar, chicken stock, fish sauce and dried chillies. Stir well until the sugar dissolves.

3 Bring to the boil over a medium-high heat, then add the prawns, garlic and shallots, and stir-fry about 3–4 minutes, or until the prawns are only just cooked. Scatter over the spring onions and serve at once.

liquid as required. Any leftover liquid can be stored in the fridge and used for another recipe.
Tamarind slices These look a little like dried apple slices. Place them in a small bowl, then pour over enough warm water to cover and leave to soak

for about 30 minutes to extract the flavour, squeeze the tamarind slices with your fingers, then strain the juice.
Tamarind concentrate or paste Mix 15ml/1 tbsp with 60–90ml/4–6 tbsp warm water. Stir until dissolved, then use as required.

Storage

Compressed tamarind and tamarind slices will keep perfectly well in a cool dry place. Jars labelled fresh tamarind, or tamarind concentrate or paste must be kept in the fridge once opened, and used within one or two months.

CURRY POWDERS AND PASTES

CURRY POWDERS

The word curry evolved from the Tamil word *kari,* meaning any food cooked in a sauce. There is little doubt that curry powder, a ready-made blend of spices, was an early convenience food, prepared for merchants, sailors and military men who had served in the East and wished to bring these exotic flavours home. In India, the spices would have been prepared in the kitchen on a daily basis.

Over the decades and centuries these spice and curry mixtures have changed and developed, as have our tastes, so that today our supermarket shelves carry a wealth of different spice mixtures from all parts of the globe.

For enthusiastic cooks it is fun and a creative challenge to make up your own curry powder. Keep experimenting until you find the balance of spicing which suits you and your family. Of course, it is perfectly possible to mix ground spices, but it is more satisfying (and more satisfactory in terms of flavour) to start with whole spices where possible.

Left: Curry powder

Dry-frying

Many whole spices benefit from being dry-fried before they are ground. This not only makes sure that no surface moisture remains, but also heightens and develops the flavour. Use a heavy-based pan, shaking it constantly so the spices do not scorch. Purists dry-fry spices separately, but they can be heated together as long as you watch them closely. All spices react differently to heat, so here are some guidelines:
Coriander seeds often provide the dominant flavour, especially in powders from Southern India and Singapore.

Shake the pan to keep the seeds on the move, and remove them from the heat when they give off a mild, sweet, orangey perfume.
Dried chillies can be roasted in a cool oven, but it is better to sear them in a heavy-based pan, where you can keep an eye on them. Place the pan over a medium heat for 2–3 minutes, until the chillies soften and puff up. Do not let them burn, or the flavour will be ruined.
Cumin seeds should be dry-fried in a pan, and will be ready for grinding when the seeds have a nutty smell.
Black peppercorns need gentle dry-frying, just to heighten the flavour.
Fenugreek needs to be watched carefully as it will become bitter if it is dry-fried for too long. It is ready when it turns brownish yellow.
Curry leaves can be dry-fried over a cool to medium heat when fresh. Grind or pound them, using a mortar and pestle, to release their characteristic flavour, then mix them with the other spices. This works well if you are making a curry powder or paste that is to be used immediately, but if it is to be kept, make up the powder, then add the whole fresh or frozen leaves just before you are ready to use it. Remove the leaves before serving the curry. Avoid using dried curry leaves if possible, as they will have lost most of their flavour.

*Right:
Curry
spices*

Simple curry powder

This Malayan Chinese spice mixture is good for poultry, especially chicken, and robust fish curries.

MAKES ABOUT 60ML/4 TBSP

2 dried red chillies
6 whole cloves
1 small cinnamon stick
5ml/1 tsp coriander seeds
5ml/1 tsp fennel seeds
10ml/2 tsp Sichuan peppercorns
2.5ml/½ tsp grated nutmeg
5ml/1 tsp ground star anise
5ml/1 tsp ground turmeric

COOK'S TIPS

• If you prefer a very hot and punchy spice mixture, then add some or all of the chilli seeds and dry-fry with the other spices.
• Ensure that you wash your hands, and the chopping board and other utensils very thoroughly after preparing chillies.
• If your skin is particularly sensitive, then you should wear rubber gloves while you are preparing the chillies.

1 Remove the seeds from the dried chillies using the point of a knife, and discard any stems.

2 Put the chillies, cloves, cinnamon, coriander, fennel seeds and Sichuan peppercorns in a heavy-based frying pan. Dry-fry the spices, tossing them frequently until they give off a rich, spicy aroma.

3 Grind the spices to a smooth powder in a mortar, using a pestle. Alternatively, use a spice grinder, or an electric coffee grinder that is reserved for blending spices.

4 Add the grated nutmeg, star anise and turmeric. Use at once or store in an airtight jar away from strong light.

CURRY PASTES

On market stalls throughout South-east Asia are mounds of pounded wet spices; lemon grass, chilli, ginger, garlic, galangal, shallots and tamarind. After purchasing meat, chicken or fish all the cook has to do is to call on the spice seller. He or she will ask a few questions: "What sort of curry is it to be? Hot or mild? How many servings?" Having ascertained the answers and perhaps exchanged a few more pleasantries (the buying of spices is a serious yet sociable affair) the appropriate quantities of each spice will be scooped on to a banana leaf and folded into a neat cone, ready to be taken home.

We may not be able to buy our ingredients in such colourful surroundings, but supermarkets stock some very good ready-made pastes, or you can make your own. By experimenting, you will find the balance of flavours you like, and can then make up one or more of your favourite mixtures in bulk.

If you grind wet spices a lot, you may wish to invest in a traditional, large oriental mortar with a rough, pitted or ridged bowl, which helps to "hold" the ingredients while they are being pounded with the pestle.

Alternatively, for speed, you can use a food processor or blender instead of a mortar and pestle. Store any surplus curry paste in plastic tubs in the freezer.

Above: Thai curry pastes

Malay spice paste for chicken rendang

This is a fairly pungent spice paste. It can be made milder by leaving out some of the chillies.

MAKES ABOUT 350G/12OZ

6 fresh red chillies, seeded and sliced
12 shallots, roughly chopped
4 garlic cloves
2.5cm/1in piece fresh turmeric root, peeled and sliced or 5ml/ 1 tsp ground turmeric
10 macadamia nuts
2.5cm/1in cube of shrimp paste (blachan), prepared
3 lemon grass stalks

1 Place the chillies, shallots, garlic, turmeric, nuts and shrimp paste (blachan) in a food processor.

2 Trim the root end from the lemon grass and slice the lower 5cm/2in of the stalk into thin slices using a sharp knife.

3 Add the lemon grass to the remaining ingredients in the food processor and process them to a fine paste, scraping down the side of the bowl once or twice during processing.

COOK'S TIP

Use the curry paste at once or spoon into a glass jar, seal it tightly and store in the fridge for up to 3 or 4 days. Alternatively, transfer the paste to a plastic tub and store in the freezer.

Thai mussaman curry paste

This hot and spicy paste is used to make the Thai version of a Muslim curry, which is traditionally made with beef, but can also be made with other meats such as chicken or lamb.

MAKES ABOUT 170G/6OZ

12 large dried red chillies
1 lemon grass stalk
60ml/4 tbsp chopped shallots
5 garlic cloves, roughly chopped
10ml/2 tsp chopped fresh galangal
5ml/1 tsp cumin seeds
15ml/1 tbsp coriander seeds
2 cloves
6 black peppercorns
5ml/1 tsp shrimp paste (blachan), prepared
5ml/1 tsp salt
5ml/1 tsp granulated sugar
30ml/2 tbsp oil

1 Remove the seeds from the dried chillies and discard. Soak the chillies in hot water for about 15 minutes.

2 Trim the root end from the lemon grass stalk and slice the lower 5cm/2in of the stalk into small pieces.

3 Place the chopped lemon grass in a dry wok and then add the chopped shallots, garlic and galangal and dry-fry for a moment or two.

4 Stir in the cumin seeds, coriander seeds, cloves and peppercorns and dry-fry over a low heat for 5–6 minutes, stirring constantly. Spoon the mixture into a large mortar.

5 Drain the chillies and add them to the mortar. Grind finely, using the pestle, then add the prepared shrimp paste (blachan), salt, sugar and oil and pound again until the mixture forms a rough paste. Use as required, then spoon any leftover paste into a jar, seal tightly and store in the fridge for up to 4 months.

COOK'S TIPS

• Preparing a double or larger quantity of paste in a food processor makes the blending of the ingredients much easier and the paste will be smoother.
• For the best results, before you start to process the ingredients, slice them up in the following order: galangal, lemon grass, fresh ginger and turmeric, chillies, nuts, shrimp paste, garlic and shallots. Add some of the oil (or coconut cream if that is to be your frying medium) to the ingredients in the food processor if the mixture is a bit sluggish. If you do this, however, remember to use less oil or coconut cream when you fry the curry paste to eliminate the raw taste of the individual ingredients before adding the meat, poultry, fish or vegetables.
• Shrimp paste (blachan) is made from fermented shrimps. It can be bought in Asian stores. Unless it is to be fried as part of a recipe, it is always lightly cooked before use. If you have a gas cooker, simply mould the shrimp paste on to the end of a metal skewer and rotate over a low to medium gas flame, or heat under the grill of an electric cooker, until the outside begins to look crusty, but not burnt.

COOKING FATS AND OILS

CHINESE: *SHI YOU*

Animal fats and vegetable oils are regarded as essential ingredients the world over, but in Asia they play a particularly important role, largely because so much of the food is fried. Animal fat or lard was historically the medium for frying (and remains so in China), but vegetable oils are valued because they can be heated to much higher temperatures without smoking, something which is essential for quick stir-frying, in which a high degree of heat is absolutely essential. Similarly, most deep-fried food also requires a high temperature in order to achieve the desired crispness.

Oil can be extracted from sources as diverse as radishes and poppies. Rape seed (canola) oil was a popular cooking medium in China until the Portuguese introduced peanuts during the 16th century.

It was not immediately appreciated that the new crop could be a source of oil, but by the 19th century peanut oil was firmly established throughout Asia, a position it continues to hold despite competition from corn oil. In Japan, sesame oil originally held sway, but Japanese cooks soon appreciated that cooking with a mixture of sesame oil and peanut oil gave better results, especially when cooking their beloved tempura (a deep-fried vegetable and seafood dish introduced by Portuguese missionaries), as the mixed oil could be heated to higher temperatures without smoking.

Coconut and palm oil are common in South-east Asia, although both are less popular than they once were, as they are high in saturated fats.

Aroma and flavour

Fats and oils all have their own distinct aroma and flavour; some are quite strong, others fairly mild. Both lamb and beef fat, for instance are more strongly flavoured than lard (pork fat) or chicken fat, while peanut oil and rape seed oil have more taste than soya, cottonseed or sunflower oils.

Culinary uses

In the East, fats and oils are mainly used as a cooking medium, but are sometimes ingredients in their own right. In some Chinese dishes, for instance, pure lard is often stirred in shortly before serving, much as Western cooks would use cream.

Left: Sunflower oil and groundnut oil

Above: Palm oil

Preparation and cooking techniques

Although many Asian recipes depend for their success on fats and oils, it is not considered appropriate for the flavour of the fat to dominate. A technique frequently employed to neutralize the flavour of an oil is to season it. The method is quite simple. While the oil is being heated, small pieces of aromatic ingredients such as fresh ginger, spring onion and garlic are added. When these have flavoured the oil, they are then removed before other ingredients are added to the wok or pan. The technique prevents the finished dish from tasting "oily".

Storage

In normal conditions, fats and oils exposed to the air gradually become rancid due to oxidation. Cooking oil should be stored in a cool, dark place. Oil that has been heated several times in a deep-fryer may acquire an unpleasant flavour. Chinese cooks heat the oil with some fresh ginger after every use to neutralize any off flavours. You may find that you have to discard the oil after using it three or four times.

FLAVOURING OILS

CHINESE: *TIAOWEI YOU*

Several types of flavouring oil are used in Asian cooking for dips and dressings, the most common one being sesame oil, but chilli oil is also popular.

SESAME OIL

MANDARIN: *ZHIMA YOU*; CANTONESE: *MA YOU*; JAPANESE: *GAMA-ABURA*

The type of sesame oil used for flavouring is quite different from the sesame oil used for cooking in India and the Middle East. In both China and Japan, the preferred oil for flavouring is a rich flavoured oil made from processed sesame seeds, which have been roasted or toasted to bring out their flavour.

Right: Toasted sesame oil

Aroma and flavour

Sesame oil from roasted seeds has a wonderfully nutty aroma and taste. It is much stronger than either walnut oil or olive oil. Blended sesame oil has a milder flavour and is much paler in colour.

Culinary uses

Because processed sesame oil smokes easily when heated, it is not really suitable for frying. It is used for salads and dipping sauces, and is added to soups or stir-fries.

Cooking techniques

Heating helps to intensify the aroma of sesame oil, but it should never be heated for too long. It is usual to add a few drops to a soup or stir-fry shortly before serving.

Storage

Always store bottled sesame oil in a cool, dark place, because it will lose its strong aroma if exposed to heat and strong light. It becomes rancid much sooner than ordinary cooking oils, so buy in small quantities.

CHILLI OIL

CHINESE: *LA YOU*; JAPANESE: *YU*

Chilli oil is made by infusing chopped dried red chillies, red chopped onions, garlic and salt in hot vegetable oil for several hours. There is also an "XO chilli oil", which is flavoured with dried

Blended sesame oil (above) and chilli oil

scallops, and is much more expensive. Chilli oil is easy to make at home; simply put about 20 seeded and chopped dried chillies in a heatproof container. Heat 250ml/8fl oz/1 cup groundnut or corn oil until it just reaches smoking point, then leave to cool for 5 minutes. Carefully pour the oil into the heatproof container and leave to stand for at least an hour or two. Strain the oil, then use as required.

Aroma and flavour

Chilli oil has a pleasant aroma with a fiery taste that is much stronger than the flavour of either chilli bean paste or chilli sauce.

Culinary uses

Chilli oil is always used as a dipping sauce, never for cooking. In some South-east Asian countries, it is used as a dressing, and it is drizzled on top of the Burmese fish soup, Mohinga. In Thai cooking, it is added to stir-fried prawns just before serving.

Storage

Store bottles of chilli oil in a cool and dark place; the oil will keep for many months in the fridge.

VINEGARS

RICE VINEGAR

MANDARIN: *MICU*; CANTONESE: *HUCK TSO*;
JAPANESE: *SU*

Vinegar fermented from rice, or distilled
from rice grains is used extensively in
oriental cooking. The former is dark
amber in colour and is referred to in
China as red or black vinegar; the latter
is clear, so is called white vinegar. The
raw ingredients used for
making rice vinegar
consist of glutinous
rice, long grain
rice, wheat,
barley, and
rice husks. It
is fermented
twice and is
matured for up to
6–7 months. Japan
has a brown rice vinegar
– *gaen mae su* – which is
dark and heady. This vinegar, which has
been likened to balsamic vinegar, is
robust yet wonderfully smooth.

*Above: Rice
vinegar*

Aroma and flavour

Red or black vinegar has a pleasant
fragrant aroma with a mild, sweetish
flavour. The distilled white vinegar is
much stronger. It smells vinegary and
tastes quite tangy and tart. Japanese
brown rice vinegar has a distinctive
sweet and sour flavour.

Using sushi vinegar

The rice that is used to make
sushi is moistened and flavoured
with a mixture of hot rice vinegar,
sugar and salt. The technique is
simple, but it is important to use
Japanese rice and good quality
vinegar. The cooked rice is spread
out in a shallow dish and the hot
vinegar mixture is added. The rice
is turned with a spatula until the
grains are coated, and the mixture
is simultaneously fanned so that it
cools quickly and develops an
attractive sheen. The rice is then
covered until it cools completely
before being moulded.

Culinary uses

There's an old Chinese
saying which goes something like
this: "On rising in the morning, first
check that you have the seven daily
necessities for the kitchen: fuel, rice,
oil, salt, soy sauce, vinegar and tea."
Vinegar has always played a vital role in
Chinese cookery, and in some parts of
the country, particularly in the north, it
is added to almost every dish as a
matter of course, although the amounts
are sometimes so minute as to be
barely detectable. Rice vinegar is an
important ingredient in the world-
renowned sweet and sour sauce, which
originated in northern China, and also
in the popular hot and sour sauce
from Sichuan.

Throughout Asia, rice vinegar also
features in Thai cucumber sauce and
dipping sauces, such as the
Vietnamese vinegar and garlic fish
sauce. It is also widely used in
preserving and pickling.

Thai cooks add rice vinegar
to several dishes, including their
famous hot and sour soup. In
Japan, rice vinegar is famously
used for sushi rice.

Cooking techniques

If rice vinegar is heated for too
long, its fragrance will be lost, the
food will taste extremely tart and
rather unpleasant. In Asian
cooking, therefore, vinegar is
generally the last item to be
stirred into a dish. It is
also important not to use
too much vinegar; in a
good sweet and sour
sauce the key ingredients
should be in perfect
balance, the sour having a
slight edge on the sweet.

Storage

Bottled rice vinegar will keep for a very
long time, provided it is not exposed to
either heat or strong light.

OTHER VINEGARS

Coconut vinegar Made from coconut
nectar or "toddy" tapped from the
flower sheaths of
mature coconut
palms, this amber
vinegar is highly
regarded in the
Philippines.
Pon vinegar This
Japanese vinegar is
made from the juice
of citrus fruit that
resemble limes.

*Coconut vinegar
(right) and pon
vinegar*

SAUCES AND PASTES

SOY SAUCE

MANDARIN: *JIANG YOU;* CANTONESE: *CHI YOU;*
JAPANESE: *SHOYU;* INDONESIAN: *KECAP;*
KETJAP; MALAY: *KICHUP; TAUYU;*
THAI: *SIEW*

Soy sauce is
made from
fermented
soya
beans,
and is
one of
Asia's most
important
contributions to
the global pantry. It
is used all over the world,
not merely as a condiment in place of
salt, but as an ingredient in a host of
home-made and manufactured foods.

Making soy sauce involves quite a
lengthy process. The soya beans are
initially cleaned, soaked until soft and
then steamed before being mixed with a
yeast culture and wheat flour. The
mixture is then fermented for up to two
years before being filtered and bottled.
There is no short cut to making soy
sauce of high quality, and while some
modern products may cost less than
others, they have inferior flavour and
should be avoided.

Aroma and flavour

There are basically three types of
Chinese soy sauce on the market. **Light
soy sauce** is the initial extraction, like
the first pressing of virgin olive oil. It
has the most delicate flavour and is
light brown in colour with a lovely
"beany" fragrance. **Dark soy sauce** is
left to mature further, and has caramel
added to it, so it is slightly sweeter and
has a much darker colour with a
powerful aroma. Then there is the
regular soy sauce, which is a blend of
the two.

There are several different types of
Japanese soy sauce too: **Usukuchi soy
sauce** is light in colour and tastes less
salty than the Chinese light soy. **Tamari**
is dark and thick with a strong flavour,
and is even less salty than the light
type. **Shoyu** is a full-flavoured sauce

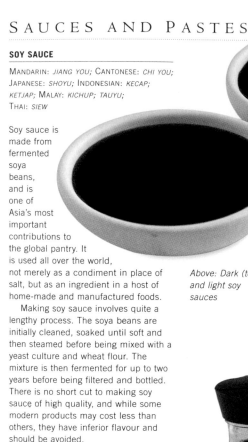

*Above: Dark (top)
and light soy
sauces*

that is aged for
up to 2 years. In
between, there is
the very popular
Kikkoman, which is a
brand name for the
equivalent of the Chinese
regular soy sauce – not too
weak, nor too strong. It is ideal
as a dipping sauce to be used at the
table, rather than for cooking.

The Indonesian **kecap manis** is thick
and black, with a powerful aroma, but
a surprisingly sweet taste. The light
variety, **kecap asin,** is quite thin and
weak, and is sometimes described as
"white soy". Indonesian cooks also
use the medium-bodied **kecap
sedang,** but this is
less popular than
kecap manis.

*Above: There is
a range of Japanese soy
sauces, from dark and thick
to lighter, less rich types.*

Above: Kecap manis (top) and kecap asin are Indonesian soy sauces

Right: Tamari sauce

Culinary uses

As a rule, light soy sauce is used for seafood, white meats, vegetables and soups, while the darker sauce is ideal for red meats, stews, barbecues and gravy. If you are serving soy sauce as a dip, choose the regular variety, or use a blend of three parts light sauce with two parts dark. This proportion also applies to marinades.

Cooking techniques

When soy sauce is used for cooking, it should be stirred in towards the end of the cooking time to avoid dulling the colour of the food, and so that the natural flavour of the principal ingredient is not overwhelmed. This point applies to soups, stews, stir-fries and quick-braised dishes, but not to slow-braised dishes, where the ingredients are simmered for a long time in a sauce that includes only a small amount of soy sauce. When soy sauce is used in a dressing for a salad or similar cold dish, the dressing should be added only just before the dish is served.

Storage

Naturally fermented soy sauce will not keep for ever; it starts to lose its aroma and flavour as soon as it is exposed to the air for any length of time. Sealed bottles can be stored for a year or two, but once the bottle has been opened, soy sauce will deteriorate fairly rapidly. Try to use it up as fast as you can, certainly before the expiry date on the label. Check the label, too, for advice on storage. Some bottles do not contain preservatives and must be kept in the fridge once opened.

Chicken Yakitori

There are several classic marinades and sauces that have soy sauce as the main ingredient. This Japanese dish uses soy sauce, which is combined with sake and sugar, and thickened with flour, as a marinade for chicken kebabs. If you like, you can make twice the quantity of sauce and reserve half to serve with the cooked kebabs.

SERVES 4

6 boneless chicken thighs, cut into chunks
bunch of spring onions, cut into short batons
Japanese seven spice powder, to serve

For the yakitori sauce
150ml/$\frac{1}{4}$ pint/$\frac{2}{3}$ cup soy sauce
90g/$3\frac{1}{2}$oz/$\frac{1}{2}$ cup caster sugar
25ml/5 tsp sake
15ml/1 tbsp plain flour

1 To make the sauce, place the soy sauce, sugar, sake and flour in a small pan and stir well. Bring to the boil, stirring all the time, then reduce the heat and simmer for 10 minutes, until the sauce in reduced by a third. Set aside.

2 Thread the chicken and spring onion pieces alternately on to 12 bamboo skewers. Grill for 5–10 minutes until the chicken is cooked through, brushing generously with the sauce once or twice during cooking.

3 Sprinkle the kebabs with Japanese seven spice powder and serve at once, with a little extra yakitori sauce, if you like.

FISH SAUCE

CHINESE: *YU LU*; THAI: *NAM PLA*;
VIETNAMESE: *NUOC MAM*

Fish sauce is an essential seasoning
for Thai and Vietnamese cooking, in
much the same way that soy sauce is
important to the Chinese and the
Japanese. In Vietnam it is often made
using shrimps, but in Thailand, the
sauce is more often made using salted,
fermented fish.

Aroma and flavour

All types of fish sauce have a pungent
flavour and aroma and are very salty.
Thai *nam pla* has a slightly stronger
flavour and aroma than the Vietnamese
or Chinese versions. The colour of fish
sauce can vary considerably; lighter-
coloured sauces are considered to be
better than darker versions.

Culinary uses

Fish sauce is used extensively
throughout Asia as a seasoning in all
kinds of savoury dishes. It is also used
to make a dipping sauce, when it is
blended with extra flavourings such as
finely chopped garlic and chillies, and
sugar and lime juice.

*Right: Fish
sauce*

Storage

Fish sauce
generally
comes in
either glass or
plastic bottles. Once opened it should
be kept in a cool, dark place where it
will keep for up to a year.

OYSTER SAUCE

MANDARIN: *HAOYOU*; CANTONESE: *HO YOW*

Oyster sauce is a Cantonese speciality.
This thick, brown, soy-based sauce is
flavoured with oyster juice, salt and
caramel, and is thickened with
cornflour. It is thicker
than soy sauce and
fish sauce, but
lighter in
colour.

Aroma and flavour

Oyster sauce has a pleasant, fragrant
aroma, and has a delicious and delicate
flavour that, surprisingly, doesn't taste
of fish at all.

Culinary uses

Oyster sauce is a highly versatile
flavouring and can be used in a wide
variety of dishes. It is especially good
with fairly bland foods, such as chicken
and beancurd, but also works very well
with more strongly flavoured ingredients
such as beef and seafood. It can be
used as a garnish and is often sprinkled
over the top of cooked dishes such as
rice and noodles.

Cooking techniques

The bottled sauce is only used as a
cooking ingredient, and it is never
served as a dip or sauce at the table.
Oyster sauce is best added to dishes
towards the end of the cooking time.

Storage

There are a number of different brands
of this sauce, and the more expensive
versions are usually far superior, and
have a much richer flavour than
cheaper versions. Once opened, the
bottle should be stored in the fridge
where the sauce will keep for a very
long time, although it is best used
before the expiry date.

*Above: Oyster
sauce*

*Above:
Dark hoisin
sauce*

*Above:
Light
hoisin sauce*

HOISIN SAUCE

MANDARIN: *HAIXIAN JIANG;* CANTONESE: *HOY SIN JIONG;* VIETNAMESE: *TUONG-DEN*

Another Cantonese speciality, hoisin is also known as barbecue sauce. Its Chinese name literally means "sea-flavour", which is a reflection on just how delicious it is, rather than an indication of its ingredients. Hoisin sauce does not contain so much as a trace of seafood, unlike oyster sauce and fish sauce.

Aroma and flavour

The main components of this very popular sauce are fermented beans, sugar, vinegar, salt, chilli, garlic and sesame oil, but there is no standard formula, so the aroma and flavour of different brands can vary considerably. A good quality product should have a fragrant aroma with a rich, warm, sweet yet salty flavour.

Culinary uses

Hoisin sauce is quite versatile and makes a valuable contribution to the kitchen. Mainly intended as a marinade, it can be used at the table as a dipping sauce, but should not accompany Peking duck as is the practice in some restaurants.

Cooking techniques

When used as a marinade, hoisin can be spooned straight from the jar over spare ribs, chicken or similar foods.

Storage

Hoisin sauce usually comes in glass jars or cans. Once opened, jars should be stored in the fridge, where the sauce will keep for several months. Canned hoisin should be decanted into non-metallic containers before being stored in the fridge.

CHILLI SAUCE

MANDARIN: *LAJIAO JIANG;* CANTONESE: *LA JYEW JYEUNG;* THAI: *SOD PRIK*

The best known Asian chilli sauce comes from China, although the Vietnamese have a very hot version and there is also a thick, spicy chilli sauce made in Thailand.

Aroma and flavour

This Chinese bottled chilli sauce is quite hot and spicy, with a touch of fruitiness, as it is made from fresh red chillies, salt, vinegar and apples or plums. The Thai version includes both hot and sweet chillies, and adds ginger, spices and vinegar. There is also a thick Chinese sauce which is made exclusively from chillies and salt. This is usually sold in jars and is much hotter than the bottled sauce.

Culinary uses

The bottled sauce is used both for cooking and as a dip, but the thicker sauce is mainly used for cooking as an alternative to chilli bean paste.

Cooking techniques

Use chilli sauce sparingly. It can be quite fiery.

Storage

Once a jar or bottle of chilli sauce has been opened it should be stored in the fridge, where it will keep almost indefinitely. Use before the expiry date.

Below: Sweet chilli sauce (top) and chilli sauce

PLUM SAUCE

MANDARIN: *MEIZI JIANG;* CANTONESE: *SHWIN MEI JIONG;* VIETNAMESE: *CUONG NGOT*

Made from plum juice with sugar, salt, vinegar and a thickening agent, plum sauce is a sort of sweet-and-sour sauce. It is generally associated with Chinese food. Thai cooks are partial to plum sauce, but they tend to make their own, using preserved plums and sugar.

Aroma and flavour

There seems to be no standard recipe for the commercially made plum sauce. The various brands all seem to use slightly different seasonings and some even add garlic, ginger or chilli to give it extra tang. Taste before use, as some brands can be quite fiery.

Culinary uses

One of the common uses for plum sauce in the West is to serve it with Peking duck. It is also used as a dip for spring rolls and other dim sum.

Storage

Plum sauce is usually sold in glass jars. One opened, the jar should be kept in the fridge.

LEMON SAUCE

MANDARIN: *NINGMENG JIANG;* CANTONESE: *NING MUNG JIONG*

Lemon sauce is one of those condiments that was especially created for the Western market. It probably originated in Hong Kong, like black bean sauce. Thick, smooth and velvety, it has an immediate appeal for the Western palate.

Aroma and flavour

The sauce has a rather piquant citrus aroma with a spicy and tangy sweet flavour. It is another sauce from the sweet-and-sour stable, but with the difference that it is made from fresh lemon juice and rind. Salt and sugar are added, and starch is used for thickening. Most brands have artificial colouring added to give the sauce a bright colour.

Above, from top: oyster, plum and hoisin sauces

Culinary uses

The use of lemon sauce in cooking seems to be limited to a single dish, lemon chicken, which is on the menu of most Cantonese restaurants. Other than that, it can be served with deep-fried food, particularly seafood.

Storage

Once opened, the bottle or jar should be stored in the fridge. The fresh flavour of the sauce may be dulled if it is kept for too long, so use it before the expiry date.

Above: Lemon sauce

BLACK BEAN SAUCE

MANDARIN: *CHIZI JIANG;* CANTONESE:
SI JIR JIONG

A mixture of puréed salted black beans with soy sauce, sugar and spice, this popular sauce is especially manufactured for the convenience of Western cooks, since people in China and South-east Asia generally use only whole fermented beans, and make their own sauce by crushing the beans in the wok while cooking.

Aroma and flavour

Fermented black beans have a powerful "fragrance" and a strong flavour that does not always appeal to the untutored Western palate, but once introduced to its rather earthy taste, many people grow to like it immensely.

Culinary uses

Black bean sauce should not be used cold straight from the jar or bottle, but should always be heated first. It is usually blended with other strongly flavoured seasonings such as spring onions, garlic, ginger and chillies before being added to stews, stir-fries, and braised or steamed dishes. Ready-made black bean sauces seasoned either with garlic or chillies are available too. These should also be heated before being used, to bring out the aroma and flavour.

Storage

Once opened, the jar should be stored in the fridge. Black bean sauce keeps extremely well.

Above:
Black bean
sauce

YELLOW BEAN SAUCE

MANDARIN: *HUANG JIANG:*
CANTONESE: *MO SHIH JIONG;*
THAI: *TAO JIEW KAOW*

Also known as brown bean sauce or ground bean sauce, this Chinese favourite consists of crushed fermented soya beans which have been mixed with salt, wheat flour and sugar to make a paste which is not only useful on its own, but is also the basis of numerous more elaborate sauces. hoisin sauce, chu hou sauce, Guilin chilli sauce, Sichuan hot sauce and Peking duck sauce all owe their ancestry to yellow bean sauce.

Aroma and flavour

Regular yellow bean sauce has a wonderfully "beany" aroma with a delectable flavour. It is not as salty as black bean sauce, and cooks in every region of China add

Left: Fermented yellow beans and yellow bean sauce

Above: Fermented black beans, which Chinese cooks use to make their own black bean sauce.

their own spices and seasonings to make individual blends.

Culinary uses

Yellow bean sauce is very versatile in the kitchen. It adds an extra dimension to most meat, poultry, fish and even some vegetable dishes, whether in stir-fries, braised dishes or roasts. It is also the ideal basis for a marinade, usually with additional ingredients such as garlic, spring onions and rice wine.

Storage

Once a can or jar of yellow bean sauce has been opened, the contents should be transferred to a lidded plastic tub and stored in the fridge. Like black bean sauce, it keeps very well.

CHILLI BEAN PASTE

MANDARIN: *DOUBAN JIANG;* CANTONESE: *TOBAN DJAN*

This is a Sichuan speciality. What makes it unique is the fact that the beans used are not soya beans, but a type of broad bean, hence the name *douban* or *toban* in Chinese. Outside China the sauce is sold under various names, including chilli bean sauce, hot bean sauce or just plain Sichuan sauce.

Aroma and flavour

There are several chilli bean pastes on the market, ranging from mild to hot, but all have a lovely "beany" aroma with a rich flavour. The genuine Pixian paste made in Sichuan is seldom seen in the West, which is a pity, for it is superior in quality to the majority of brands made in Hong Kong, Taiwan or Singapore.

Above: Chilli bean paste

Right: Red bean paste

Miso

This is the collective name for several types of soya bean paste, made from steamed soya beans fermented with various natural yeasts. Some of these starter moulds are based upon rice, others on wheat or barley, and yet more on soya beans themselves. The pastes come in different colours, textures and flavours, depending on the yeast used and the length of the

fermentation process. Red or *mugi* miso (*below centre*), the most popular paste, is more strongly flavoured than the sweeter white *kome* miso (*below left*). A third type, *hacho* miso (*below right*), is dark with a strong flavour. Miso is the key ingredient in a soup served at almost every Japanese meal. When mixed with mayonnaise it makes the increasingly popular miso-mayo.

Culinary uses

Chilli bean paste and chilli sauce are not interchangeable; each has its own distinct flavour and consistency. Chilli bean paste is slightly thicker than chilli sauce and is an indispensable seasoning in Sichuan cooking. It is used to add flavour to stir-fries and braised dishes.

Cooking techniques

Chilli bean paste must be thoroughly heated before being used and should never be served cold at the table as a dipping sauce.

Storage

Once opened, the jar should be stored in the fridge. Chilli bean paste keeps well, but should be used before the expiry date on the jar.

RED BEAN PASTE

MANDARIN: *DOUSHA;* CANTONESE: *DOW SA*

Made from either red kidney beans or aduki beans, this is a thick, smooth paste, which is sweetened with rock sugar. The paste comes in small cans and is only available from Asian and oriental stores.

Aroma and flavour

The paste has a pleasant, mild fragrance with a subtle flavour. Although it is sweetened, the sauce is never cloying, and oriental cooks often add extra sugar to intensify the flavour. Occasionally, other flavourings such as essence of sesame seeds or ground cassia are blended in.

Culinary uses

Red bean paste is mainly used in sweet dishes and is a popular filling for cakes and steamed buns. It is also spread on pancakes, which are then deep-fried.

Storage

Once the can has been opened, the contents should be transferred to a sealed plastic tub and stored in the fridge, where the paste will keep for several months. Make a note of the use-by date on the can.

Left: Shrimp paste

until the aroma is very pungent. The colour of the paste can be anything from oyster pink to purplish brown, depending upon the type of shrimp and the precise process used. It is compressed and sold in block form or packed in tiny tubs or jars.

SHRIMP PASTE

MALAY: *BLACHAN; BALACHAN;* INDONESIAN: *TERASI; TRASSI;* THAI: *KAPI;* BURMESE: *NGAPI*

Whether you call it *blachan, terasi, kapi* or *ngapi*, shrimp paste is an essential ingredient in scores of savoury dishes throughout South-east Asia. It is made from tiny shrimps which have been salted, dried, pounded and then left to ferment in the hot humid conditions

Sesame paste
The sesame paste used in oriental cooking is not the same as tahini, the ingredient that frequently crops up in recipes from the Middle East. Whereas tahini is made from raw sesame seeds, sesame paste is derived from seeds which have been dry-fried or roasted to bring out the rich nutty flavour. If an oriental recipe calls for sesame paste, don't be tempted to try tahini, therefore. Instead, use peanut butter with a little sesame oil stirred in to approximate the correct flavour.

Aroma and flavour
There's no disguising the origin of this paste. The moment you unwrap it or lift the lid, the smell of rotten fish is quite overwhelming. Do not let this put you off, however. The odour vanishes when the paste is cooked, and this is one of those ingredients that really does make a difference to the food, contributing depth, pungency and a recognizable South-east Asian signature.

Culinary uses
Shrimp paste is good source of protein and vitamin C. It is used to flavour rice dishes, is stirred into satay sauces and gives depth to salad dressings, dipping sauces, curries and braised dishes. It is the key ingredient in the famous *nam prik*, a dipping sauce whose other ingredients include garlic, chillies and fish sauce, and which appears as a condiment at almost every Thai meal. Burmese cooks use it to intensify the flavour of *balachaung*, a spicy dried shrimp mixture forked into rice.

Preparation
Before using shrimp paste in a sambal, dressing or salad, it is necessary to heat it to temper the raw flavour (see right).

Storage
If you buy the paste in block form, store it in a screwtop jar in a cool place. It will keep for several months. Jars of paste should be kept in the fridge.

Preparing shrimp paste
Shrimp paste can be used straight from the packet if it is to be fried with other ingredients, but it needs to be heated to temper its raw taste before using in sambals, dressings and salads.

1 Cut off a small piece of shrimp paste and shape it into a 1cm/½in cube. Mould the paste on to the end of a metal skewer.

2 Holding the end of the skewer in an oven glove, rotate the paste over a low to medium gas flame, or under an electric grill until the outside begins to look dry, but not burnt. This method works well, but gives off a very strong smell.

3 Alternatively, to avoid the strong smell, wrap the cube of paste in a piece of foil and dry-fry in a frying pan for about 5 minutes, turning it occasionally.

SAMBALS

In the West, sambals have come to mean the side dishes served with a curry, but this is several steps away from the original South-east Asian term, which was, and still is, applied to a number of hot, spicy relishes, sauces and similar accompaniments that are based on chillies. Sambals are particularly popular in Indonesia, and feature strongly in the famous *Rijstafel*, a veritable feast which includes dozens of different dishes, and which was developed in the days when Indonesia was still the Dutch East Indies. Thanks to the connection, *Rijstafel* is also well known and loved in the Netherlands, and bottled sambals are widely available in that country.

In Indonesia, a sambal can also be a main dish. *Sambal goreng*, for instance is a spicy chilli sauce, which may include a variety of foods such as tiny meat balls, cubes of fish, wedges of hard-boiled eggs or vegetables.

Culinary uses

In Malaysia, Singapore and Indonesia *sambal blachan* (chilli and shrimp paste sambal) is a favourite. Fresh red chillies are roughly chopped, then pounded with a little salt and prepared shrimp paste *(blachan)*. A little lime or lemon juice is added to the mixture to loosen it slightly. *Sambal blachan* is extremely hot – especially when the seeds have been left in the chillies – so deserves to be served with a health warning! *Sambal oelek* is similar, but a little brown sugar is added to the chopped chillies to bring out the flavours. Sometimes labelled "chopped chilli", this product is now sold in jars in many supermarkets. One teaspoonful (5ml) is equivalent to 1 small chilli. After use, the jar should be closed tightly and kept in the fridge.

At a typical Thai meal there may be one or two sambals in addition to the much loved *nam prik,* a combination of dried prawns, shrimp paste (blachan), garlic, chillies, fish sauce, lemon juice and brown sugar. *Nam prik* complements raw, steamed, fried or boiled vegetables and is often simply stirred into a bowl of plain boiled or steamed Thai rice. Another popular sambal is made from fish sauce, lemon juice, shallots and chillies; a blend that enhances all kinds of fish and seafood dishes.

Sambal oelek

This chilli sambal will keep for about 6 weeks in a sealed jar in the fridge, so it is worth making up a reasonable quantity at a time if you frequently cook Indonesian-style dishes. Use a stainless steel or plastic spoon to measure out the sauce as required. This sauce is fiercely hot, and it will irritate the skin, so should you get any on your fingers, immediately wash them well in soapy water.

MAKES ABOUT 350G/12 OZ

450g/1lb fresh red chillies
10ml/2 tsp salt

1 Cut the chillies in half, scrape out the seeds using the point of a sharp knife and discard with the stalks. Plunge the chillies into a pan of boiling water and cook them for 5–8 minutes.

2 Drain the chillies, then place them in the bowl of a food processor or blender and process until finely chopped. The paste should be fairly coarse, so stop processing before it gets too smooth.

3 Spoon the paste into a glass jar, stir in the salt and cover with a piece of greaseproof paper or clear film before screwing on the lid.

4 Store the sambal in the fridge. Spoon it into small dishes to serve as an accompaniment, or use it as suggested in recipes.

Left: Sambal oelek (left), sambal blachan (front) and nam prik *sauce are very hot chilli sauces.*

Below: Nuoc cham

family meal pieces of cooked meat, fish or vegetables may be dipped into a communal bowl or a tiny spoonful of the sambal may be put on each diner's plate, but on special occasions small individual dishes are used. These little dishes are sold in many Asian stores and oriental supermarkets.

Preparation

For the freshest flavours mix the sambal ingredients just before serving. Use a food processor or blender to blend the wet ingredients and a pestle and mortar to grind the dry ingredients.

Storage

Any leftover sambals are best stored in a glass jar in the fridge. Before putting on the lid, cover the jar with a piece of greaseproof paper or clear film to protect the lid from corrosion.

In Vietnam the salt and pepper of the Western table is replaced by *nuoc cham*. This is a piquant sambal made from, chillies, garlic, sugar, lime juice or rice vinegar, and fish sauce and is the classic combination of hot, sweet, sour and salt flavours that is so typical of Vietnamese cooking.

Sambals and sauces are usually served in small bowls or saucers. At a

---

Nuoc cham

This spicy Vietnamese sambal makes a delicious, if fiery, dipping sauce and is good served with crisp, fried spring rolls.

MAKES ABOUT 105ML/7 TBSP

2 fresh red chillies, seeded
2 garlic cloves, crushed
15ml/1 tbsp sugar
45ml/3 tbsp fish sauce
juice of 1 lime or ½ lemon

1 Place the chillies in a large mortar and pound to a paste using a pestle.

2 Transfer the chillies to a bowl and add the garlic, sugar and fish sauce. Stir in lime or lemon juice to taste.

COOK'S TIP

Be careful, when handling either fresh or dried chillies; they contain capsaicin, an oily substance which can cause intense irritation to sensitive skin, so wash your hands thoroughly after handling them, or wear rubber gloves. And do not touch or rub your eyes.

Sambal kecap

This Indonesian sauce or sambal can be served as a dip for satays instead of the usual peanut sauce, particularly with beef and chicken, and it is also very good with pieces of deep-fried chicken.

MAKES ABOUT 150ML/¼ PINT/⅔ CUP

1 fresh red chilli, seeded and
finely chopped
2 garlic cloves, crushed
60ml/4 tbsp dark soy sauce
20ml/4 tsp lemon juice or 15ml/
1 tbsp tamarind juice
30ml/2 tbsp hot water
30ml/2 tbsp deep-fried onion slices
(optional)

1 Place the chopped chilli, crushed garlic, soy sauce, and lemon juice or tamarind juice in a small bowl with the hot water and mix together well.

2 Stir in the deep-fried onion slices, if using, and leave the sambal to stand at room temperature for about 30 minutes before serving.

Sambal blachan

Serve this hot and pungent sambal as an accompaniment to rice meals.

MAKES ABOUT 30ML/2 TBSP

2–4 fresh red chillies, seeded
salt
1cm/½in cube of shrimp paste
(blachan)
juice of ½ lemon or lime

1 Place the chillies in a mortar, add a little salt and pound them to a paste using a pestle.

2 Cut off a small piece of shrimp paste (blachan) and shape it into a 1cm/½in cube. Mould the paste on to the end of a metal skewer.

3 Holding the end of the skewer in a cloth or oven glove, rotate the paste over a low gas flame, or under an electric grill until the outside begins to look dry, but not burnt.

4 Add the shrimp paste to the chillies and pound to mix well. Add lemon or lime juice to taste.

PRESERVED AND PICKLED VEGETABLES

Preserved and pickled food plays an important part in the oriental diet. In the days before refrigeration and rapid transportation, fresh food had to be preserved for the lean months, and so that it could be conveyed to regions that were often a long way from the source of supply.

Preserved and pickled vegetables and, to a lesser extent, fruit are used all over Asia. Some of the more famous examples include *chow chow,* the Chinese sweet mixed pickles that are now an American favourite, and *kimchee,* the tart, garlicky pickle that is served at almost every Korean meal. In Japan, pickled vegetables are hugely popular, as are pickled plums, while Indonesian cooks relish *atjar kuning,* a yellow mixed pickle which is mildly hot.

There are several ways of preserving and pickling food. The most common way is to use salt as a preservative, then dry the food in the sun or by another source of heat. Another age-old method is to partially dry the food, then pickle it in brine or a soy-based solution.

Below: Pickled mustard greens

Below: A selection of Chinese pickles

SICHUAN PRESERVED VEGETABLE

MANDARIN: *ZHACAI;* CANTONESE: *JA CHOI*

This pickle, made from the stems of mustard cabbage, originated in Sichuan province, but is now made in other parts of China. The stems are dried in the sun, then pickled in brine. After being trimmed and cleaned, they are pressed to extract excess liquid (the Mandarin name *zhacai* means "pressed vegetable"), before being blended with chillies and spices, and stored in sealed urns to mature.

Aroma and flavour

Sichuan preserved vegetable has a pungent aroma that may not appeal to the uninitiated. It has a smooth and crunchy texture and tastes quite salty and peppery.

Culinary uses

Unlike most other types of preserved and pickled vegetables, Sichuan preserved vegetable is a very versatile ingredient. It is not merely served raw as a relish, but is also cooked with other foods in stir-fries, soups and steamed dishes.

Preparation and cooking techniques

Because of its strong hot and salty flavour, Sichuan preserved vegetable is often rinsed in water to remove some of the excess salt and chillies before it is finely sliced or shredded for use.

Storage

Sichuan preserved vegetable is normally sold in cans, although you may be able to buy the pickle loose in some oriental stores. Any unused pickle should be transferred to an airtight container and stored in the fridge, where it will keep almost indefinitely.

CHINESE PICKLES

There is a wide range of Chinese pickles available in the West. Some appear in packets, some in jars, and some in cans. A pickle may consist of a single ingredient such as ginger, garlic, spring onion bulbs, chillies, cabbage, cucumber, gourd, runner beans, bamboo shoots, carrots or daikon (Chinese radish or mooli) or a mixture. Individual items are generally pickled in a dark soy solution, while mixed vegetables tend to be pickled in clear brine to which sugar, Sichuan

Below: Cucumbers are a popular pickled vegetable in many Asian countries. These are from Korea.

peppercorns, distilled spirit and fresh ginger have been added, with chillies and vinegar as optional ingredients. The cleaned vegetables are pickled in the solution in a sealed earthenware urn. This is left in a cool, dark place for at least a week in summer, or up to a month in winter. The longer the pickling process, the better the taste.

JAPANESE PICKLES

JAPANESE: *TSUKEMONO*

There are many varieties of the Japanese pickles known as *tsukemono*. The vegetables that are used are more or less the same as those used in China, but the method of pickling is somewhat different. To start with, instead of earthenware urns, only

Below: Chow chow – Chinese sweet mixed pickles

wooden barrels are used in Japan and, instead of being pickled in a brine solution, the vegetables are layered with salt. When the barrel is full, a lid is put on top, and this is weighted down with a large stone or similar weight. The combined effect of the salt and the compression forces the liquid out of the vegetables and they are pickled in their own juices.

Other methods include pickling in sake, miso or rice bran, and the most popular types of vegetable used are daikon (mooli), bok choy, cucumber, aubergine, horseradish and the bulbs of spring onions. Thinly sliced pink pickled ginger (gari) is traditionally served with sushi and sashimi.

Japanese pickles form an essential part of a meal. They are served as a relish to accompany the cooked food, as well as a dessert or a means of cleansing the palate at the end. They are either served singly or in groups of two or three, always beautifully arranged in small individual dishes.

Umeboshi These small pickled plums (below) are a particular Japanese delicacy. The plums are picked before they are ripe and are pickled in salt, with red shiso leaves to give them their distinctive colour. They have a sharp and salty taste and are often chopped and used as a filling for rice balls.

Pickled bamboo shoots A delicacy in Vietnam, this consists of sliced bamboo shoots in spiced vinegar. The shoots are quite sour and should be soaked in water to remove some of the bitterness. They are mainly used in soups and stocks, and are often served with duck.

Pickled garlic This is a favourite in Thailand. The small bulbs are pickled whole in a sweet and sour brine (below).

Pickled limes Whole limes preserved in brine or a mixture of soy sauce, sugar, salt and vinegar are another Thai speciality.

COCONUT MILK AND CREAM

Coconut milk is an essential ingredient in South-east Asian cooking. There is an old saying that "he who plants a coconut palm, plants food and drink, vessels and clothing, a habitation for himself and a heritage for his children". Once mature, the palms will go on producing coconuts for 75–100 years, which helps to explain why they are so highly prized.

The coconut was called the nut of India until the Portuguese, struck by its appearance, changed its name to "coco", meaning clown or monkey. Fresh coconuts are available at certain times of the year in oriental stores and supermarkets. The liquid you can hear sloshing about inside the nut when it is shaken is coconut juice, not coconut milk. As any traveller who has tasted it will attest, the juice makes a refreshing drink, especially when tapped from a fresh green coconut. It can also be made into palm wine, which can be pretty potent.

An average size coconut weighs about 675g/1½lb. If it is fresh, it will be full of liquid, so test by shaking well before buying. To open a coconut, hold

Below: A fresh coconut will break neatly into two pieces if you hit it in just the right place.

Below: Coconut milk

it in the palm of your left hand, with the "eyes" just above your thumb. The fault line runs between the eyes. Hold the coconut over a bowl to catch the juice, then carefully strike the line with the unsharpened side of a cleaver or a hammer. If you have done this correctly, the coconut will break neatly into two pieces. Taste a little of the white flesh to make sure that the coconut is fresh, as on rare occasions the flesh may have become rancid. Slip a palette knife between the outer husk and the flesh and prize out the pieces of fresh

coconut. The thin brown skin on these pieces can be removed with a potato peeler, if you like.

Coconut milk and cream are both made from the grated flesh of the coconut, and in the East, it is possible to buy bags of freshly grated coconut for just this purpose. Warm water is added and the coconut is squeezed repeatedly until the mixture is cloudy and has a wonderful coconut flavour. When strained, this is coconut milk. If the milk is left to stand, coconut cream will float to the surface in much the same way as regular cream does on whole milk.

Coconut milk is now available in cartons and cans, and even in countries with a plentiful supply of coconuts cooks often use these products for convenience and speed. The quality is excellent, and it is even possible to buy a version that is 88 per cent fat free.

Creamed coconut comes in 200g/7oz blocks. This is a very useful product, as small quantities can be cut off and added to dishes to supply a little richness just before serving. When a very small quantity of coconut milk is called for dissolve 50g/2oz creamed coconut in 100ml/3½fl oz/scant ½ cup hot water.

Above: Creamed coconut block

Coconut cream can be made in the same way, but the amount of creamed coconut should be increased to 75g/3oz. Ready-to-use coconut cream comes in cartons and is a magical ingredient where a rich coconut aroma and flavour are required. In many Thai curries the spices are initially fried in bubbling coconut cream instead of the more usual oil.

Culinary uses

Coconut is widely used in South-east Asian cooking. The milk is used as a cooking medium instead of stock in a variety of dishes, and it is also added at the end of cooking to enrich stews and curries. It can be cooked with rice, to make a savoury accompaniment, or as the basis for rice cakes, and also to make a delicious creamy rice pudding. In Thailand, coconut milk is often used to make aromatic soups.

Below: Coconut cream

Making coconut milk

Coconut milk can be made at home, from desiccated coconut. Although the procedure takes a little time, it has plenty of advantages. Desiccated coconut is readily available and is an item that many cooks routinely stock in their store cupboards. You can make as much or as little as you like – although the method is more practical for large quantities – and coconut milk made this way is less expensive than any of the alternatives.

2 Place a sieve lined with muslin over a large bowl in the sink. Ladle some of the softened coconut into the muslin.

1 Tip 225g/8oz/2⅔ cups desiccated coconut into the bowl of a food processor and pour over 450ml/ ¾ pint/scant 2 cups boiling water. Process for 20–30 seconds and allow to cool a little. If making several batches transfer immediately to a large bowl and repeat.

3 Bring up the ends of the cloth and twist it over the sieve to extract as much of the liquid as possible. Discard the spent coconut. Use the coconut milk as directed in recipes.

COOK'S TIPS

• When making coconut milk, instead of discarding the spent coconut, it can be re-used to make a second batch of coconut milk. This will be of a poorer quality and should only be used to extend a good quality first quantity of coconut milk.
• Any unused coconut milk or cream can be transferred to a plastic tub and stored in the fridge for a day or two, or poured into a freezer container and frozen for use on another occasion.
• Before using newly made coconut milk, leave it to stand for 10 minutes or more, and the coconut cream will float to the top. Skim off the cream using a large spoon if needed, or leave it to enrich the milk.

BEER, WINE AND SPIRITS

The art of making alcoholic beverages is an ancient one. Man has been making alcoholic drinks ever since the discovery that a grain and water mash would ferment if left to stand, producing a sour brew that would intoxicate.

Archaeological finds in northern China provide evidence that the Chinese were using separate drinking cups and bowls for different beverages as long ago as the 22nd century BC. Historians

Below: Leading Japanese beers include Sapporo and Asahi, both of which are widely available in the West.

agree that a considerable length of time must have elapsed from the beginning of the making and drinking of a primitive type of "wine" to the sophistication of using vessels in a variety of shapes for specific purposes, so the Chinese may well have been imbibing some form of alcoholic beverage at the dawn of their civilization more than 5,000 years ago. By the time of the Shang Dynasty (c. 1600–1100 BC), a dark wine

Above: Chinese beers include Five Star beer and the light Pilsener, Tsingtao.

was being brewed from millet, and was ceremonially served in elaborate bronze drinking vessels.

A new development in the art of brewing was achieved during the early part of the 12th century BC, where textual evidence records that a form of barm or leaven was used in wine-making. With this discovery, the Chinese were able to control both the flavour and alcoholic content of a variety of wines made from different fruits and grains. Wine continues to be an important drink, although its popularity has now been overtaken by beer.

BEER

MANDARIN: *PI JIU*; CANTONESE: *PI CHIEW*

Beer brewing was not introduced into China and Japan until towards the end of the 19th century, but it rapidly became an extremely popular drink. Today, beer is the favourite alcoholic beverage in Asia, and almost every country in the region has breweries producing beers for export as well as for domestic consumption.

The style of beer most favoured by Asian drinkers is a bottom-fermented brew in the style of Pilsener (Pils), a pale, golden-coloured lager with a characteristically well-hopped palate and 4.5–5 per cent alcohol by volume.

Chinese beers

Without doubt, the best known Chinese beer is **Tsingtao**, a light, dry Pilsener-type beer which is brewed from the sweet spring water of Laoshan, using

Chinese barley and hops. It has a refreshing and delicate taste, and enjoys a huge popularity abroad, not just with expatriate Chinese, but among Westerners as well.

In 1898, part of the Shandong Peninsula was ceded to Germany as a colony. Besides the winery in Yantai, the Germans also established a brewery at Tsingtao in 1903, which was called the

Below: Singaporean Tiger beer is popular all over the world.

Anglo-German Brewery Company. Because of the vicissitudes of history, it went through a number of different owners – Britain, Germany and Japan – until after World War II, when it was taken over by the People's Republic of China. Since then a number of breweries have been established all over China, but Tsingtao Brewery remains the largest and most productive brewer in the land.

Other brands that can occasionally be seen in the West are **Beijing Beer**, **Shanghai Beer**, **Snowflake** and **Yu Chuan** ("Jade Spring") **Beer**. These all are Pilsener-type lagers, each with their own individual flavour.

Japanese beers

The huge beer industry of Japan also owes its origins to foreign investment. In 1869, the American firm of Wiegrand and Copeland started an experimental brewery at Yokohama. Soon afterwards, the Japanese Government sent a researcher to Germany to acquire technical know-how, and subsequently the Copeland operation was passed to Japanese management, taking the name Kirin in 1888.

Today, the Kirin Brewery Company has became one of the biggest brewers in the world. It is part of Japan's Mitsubishi conglomerate, and its output even surpasses that of Heineken. Kirin has nine breweries in different parts of Japan, and **Kirin Beer** is exported to almost every country in the world. It used to enjoy 60 per cent of domestic sales, but has recently been pushed down to about 40 per cent, partly owing to the surge of its chief rival **Asahi Beer**, which has rapidly increased its export market in recent years. Other strong contenders for the crown of the

Left: Canned Thai beer

Japanese beer industry are **Sapporo Beer**, which also challenges Kirin's claim of being the oldest brewer; and the newcomer **Suntory Beer**, which only started brewing in 1963.

South-east Asian beers

The world-renowned **Tiger Beer** of Singapore came into being by accident. The breweries were established after Heineken failed to reach an agreement with the Dutch Colonial Government to set up their breweries in Java in 1929, so established the Malayan Breweries in Singapore and later in Kuala Lumpur instead. Tiger Beer is now brewed by Asia Pacific Breweries of Singapore, and has achieved worldwide sales figures envied by all its competitors.

From Thailand, the biggest selling lager is **Singha**, brewed by Boon Rawd Brewery. The name Singha is a reference to the elegant but fearsome lion-like creature of local mythology.

Perhaps not that many people are aware that the Philippines is the home of one of the world's major brewing groups – **San Miguel**. This group has three breweries in the Philippines, one in Hong Kong, and one in Papua New Guinea. Outside of Asia, San Miguel has three breweries in Spain, but ironically these are only offshoots of its headquarters in the Philippines.

Dutch colonial links are still evident in Indonesia, where **Heineken** eventually did establish an associate company in Java to produce a Pilsener-style beer. Elsewhere in Asia, popular beers include the Vietnamese **"33"**; **Taiwan Beer** from Taiwan; and **OB** and **Crown** from Korea, but these are seldom seen in the West.

WINE

MANDARIN: *JIU;* CANTONESE: *CHIEW*

In contrast to their sophisticated approach to food, the Chinese, as a whole, are remarkably indiscriminating when it comes to alcoholic beverages. Unless they are connoisseurs, the Chinese often fail to distinguish between table wine, in which the alcoholic content is low, and distilled spirits, in which it is high. In everyday usage, the Chinese character *jiu* or *chiew* means any alcoholic beverage.

Chinese wines

As can be expected in a country where rice is the staple food, rice wine leads the field. There are hundreds of different varieties of rice wine in China, but only a few of these are exported.

Chinese rice wine is generally known as **huang jiu** (yellow wine) in Chinese, because of its golden amber colour. The best known and best quality rice wine is **Shao Xing**, named after the district where it is made. Shao Xing, or Shao Hsing is situated south of Hangzhou in Zhejiang province, and its wine-making history dates back to 470 BC. The main grains used for making Shao Xing are glutinous rice, millet and ordinary rice, and the water comes from a large lake

Left: Sake

Below: Shao Xing

Above: Glutinous rice wine

which is fed by the fountains and streams that flow down the sandy mountains on one side, and the dense bamboo-forested hills on the other. The water is so clear and the surface so smooth that the lake is known locally as "the mirror".

There are several varieties of Shao Xing wines, ranging in colour from golden amber to dark brown, and in the percentage of alcohol by volume from 14–16 per cent. The aroma is always quite distinctive, smelling subtly fragrant and smoky. Shao Xing should be drunk warm, and always with food. It is also used in cooking, and is added to the food towards the end of the cooking time so that the aroma is retained. One of the most famous Shao Xing wines is **Hua Tiao**, meaning "carved flower". This is a reference to the pretty patterns carved on the urns in which the wine is stored in underground cellars to mature.

As in beer brewing and whisky distilling, what distinguishes Shao Xing rice wine from all its imitators is the water used, which just cannot be replicated elsewhere. So beware of Shao

Xing/Hsing wine made in Taiwan, which pales, literally, by comparison. Read the small print on the label; if it says "made in ROC (Republic of China)" it is a fake.

China also produces some quite good grape wines. Several of these are exported to the West. The names to look for are **Dynasty**, **Great Wall** and **Huadong**. The whites (Riesling and Chardonnay) seem to be more successful than the red Cabernet Sauvignon. China may well become an important wine region in the future.

Mirin

This is a sweet rice wine with a low alcohol content. It is widely used in cooking, and is usually added towards the end, so that the subtle flavour is retained. Mirin is now available in the West. If you cannot locate it, dry sherry can be used instead, but the results will not be the same.

Pears with Chinese White Wine, Star Anise and Ginger

Star anise and ginger complement these sweet, wine-poached pears.

SERVES 4

75g/3oz/6 tbsp caster sugar
300ml/½ pint/1¼ cups white wine
thinly pared rind and juice of
   1 lemon
7.5cm/3in piece fresh root ginger,
   bruised
5 star anise
10 cloves
600ml/1 pint/2½ cups cold water
6 slightly unripe pears
25g/1oz stem ginger, sliced
natural yogurt, to serve

1 Place the caster sugar, wine, lemon rind and juice, fresh root ginger, star anise, cloves and water into a large pan. Bring to the boil.

2 Meanwhile, peel the pears. Add them to the wine mixture and ensure that they are covered in liquid, then lower the heat. Cover and simmer for 15 minutes or until the pears are tender.

3 Lift out the pears with a slotted spoon and keep them warm. Boil the wine syrup until reduced by half, then pour over the pears. Cool, then chill. Slice the pears and arrange on serving plates. Remove the root ginger from the sauce and add the stem ginger, then spoon the sauce over the pears.

Japanese wines

It is widely known that **sake** is the national drink of Japan. There are many varieties of this rice-based brew, but only a few are exported to the West. Unlike Chinese rice wine, sake is almost colourless, and it tastes slightly sweeter. It usually has an alcohol content of about 15 per cent. Like Chinese rice wine, sake should be drunk with food. Most types of sake are served warm, with the exception of **Ginjo**, a fine, dry wine which is invariably served chilled.

The traditional way of serving sake is in a porcelain jug, which is immersed in hot water until the wine is judged to be at the right temperature for serving. It is then poured into small cups. The host

lifts a cup in both hands and passes it to his guest with a courteous bow. The cup must not be passed in one hand, as this shows disrespect. Having received the cup, also in both hands, the guest bows and downs the warm wine in one swift movement.

Good quality grape wines are also produced in Japan, but the output is quite small, owing to the scarcity of land available for growing vines and the extreme climate, all of which make wine-making difficult.

The three big names are **Suntory**, **Mercian** and **Mann's**. All these companies produce both white and red wines, but very little of the wine output is exported overseas.

SPIRITS

Chinese spirits

The Chinese name for distilled spirit –
bai jiu – means "white wine" and stems
from the fact that it is colourless, as
opposed to the "yellow" rice wine.
Asking for white wine in China can,
therefore, lead to some interesting and
potentially disastrous social occasions,
as most Chinese spirits have an alcohol
content of over 50 per cent.

Most Chinese spirits are distilled
from a variety of grains, the commonest
of these is sorghum, which is a cross
between rice and millet. China has far
more distilled spirits than wines, and

*Below: Mou-Tai, which is served at state
banquets, and Chu Yeh Ching*

CHU YEH CHING
CHINESE LIQUEUR

some of the spirits are blended with
herbs for use as medicinal tonics.

Mou-Tai is undoubtedly China's top
spirit, and it is used for toasts at state
banquets and other celebrations. It may
be an acquired taste, but it was
awarded a medal at the 1915
International Trade Fair in Panama,
second only to France's cognac, but
ahead of Scotch whisky as the world's
top three spirits. Mou-Tai, which means
"thatched terrace", is the name of a
village in Kweichow in south-west
China. The world-renowned spirit is
distilled from two grains, wheat and
sorghum, with the water taken from
the stream running through a nearby
gorge. The climate is moist and warm,
and the thin layer of mist that hovers
permanently over the fast-running
stream is supposed to give the spirit its
distinctive features.

Traditionally, good rice wines came
from south China, while the best spirits
were historically produced in the north.
Although the distillery in Mou-Tai was
established in 1529, the spirit was
relatively indifferent until 1704, when a
salt merchant from Shanxi in north
China visited the area and was so
enchanted by the beauty of the village
that he decided to settle down there.
Seeking new employment, he
discovered the local spirit and set about
improving it, employing the techniques
of distilling the famous Fen Chiew from
his native northern province. Mou-tai
was the result.

Fen Chiew – the inspiration for Mou-
Tai – is one of a small group of Chinese
spirits that are available in the West. It
comes from the "apricot blossoms
village" of Shanxi province in north
China, and is distilled from millet and
sorghum with the water from a tributary
of the Yellow River. Fen Chiew has a
history of well over fifteen hundred
years, and has afforded inspiration for
many of China's greatest poets. This
spirit also forms the basis for the
famous **Chu Yeh Ching** ("bamboo leaf
green"), a medicinal liqueur which is
blended with no fewer than twelve
different herbs, including bamboo
leaves, which give it a lovely, pale
green hue. The liqueur tastes quite
refreshing despite being 47 per cent
alcohol by volume.

Other popular Chinese spirits are **Wu
Liang Ye** ("five-grain liqueur") from
Sichuan; **Mei Kuei Lu** ("rose dew"); **Wu
Chia Pi** ("five-layer skin"); and **Dong
Chiew** ("mellow wine"). All of these are
quite heady, as they are usually more
than 50 per cent proof.

China also produces Western-style
brandy, whisky, vodka, rum and gin, but
all these drinks are mainly sold for
home consumption.

Japanese spirits

Japan has its own spirit distilled from
sake called **Shochu** ("burnt wine"). It is
quite rough, and is usually diluted with
warm water for drinking, even though its
alcohol content is only about 25 per
cent by volume. Japan produces a

Above: Suntory whisky

Above: Suntory malt whisky

Other Asian spirits

Taiwan produces many of the mainland Chinese drinks as well as the Japanese-inspired **Shokushu** rice spirit. In Korea, look out for **Ginseng Ju**, which comes with what appears to be a parsnip, but is actually a large ginseng root, in every bottle. In the East Indies, the island states in the South China Sea, the local **arrack** or **raki** is crudely distilled from either coconut palm juice or sugar cane molasses. A common practice is to add rice to the fermenting base juice to boost the alcohol content of the spirit. The result is a drink that bears a strong resemblance to rum, and is often sold as such to unwary tourists.

Below: Ginseng Ju

really good quality whisky, however. The first distillery was established in 1923, and in recent years Japanese whisky has attracted considerable attention on the international market. The model for Japan's whiskies is single malt Scotch, but there are equally successful spirits made in the idiom of blended Scotch. Some distilleries blend the home-grown product with imported Scotch malt whisky.

Suntory is the biggest and best-known brand name. Several different labels are marketed worldwide, including **The Whisky**, **Excellence**, **Royal**, **Special Reserve**, **Old**, **Kakubin**, **Gold Label**, **Gold 1000**, **White Label**, **Red Label**, **Torys Extra** and **Rawhide**, which

has a bourbon flavour. Suntory's rivals in terms of whisky production are Nikka distilleries (**G & G**, **Super Nikka**, **Black Nikka** and **Hi Nikka**); Kirin Seagram (**Robert Brown** and **Dunbar**); and Sanraku Ocean (**White Label**). Several other distillers and blenders make Japanese whisky, but they only have a very small output. Perhaps the best known of these is **Godo Shusei**.

Suntory also makes good brandy. The leading brands are **Imperial**, **XO**, **VSOP**, **VSO** and **VO**. Liqueurs include **Midori**, a green, melon-flavoured liqueur; **Ocha**, a green tea liqueur with a delicate tea fragrance; and the **Creme de Kobai**, a pale pink liqueur made from Japanese plums.

SHOPPING FOR ASIAN FOODS

UK

Chinese

Good Harvest
  Fish Market
14 Newport Place
London WC2H 7PR
Tel: 020 7437 0712

Golden Gate
  Cake Shop
13 Macclesfield Street
London W1V 7LH
Tel: 020 7287 9862

Golden Gate Supermarket
16 Newport Place
London WC2H 7JS
Tel: 020 7437 6266

Golden Gate
  Hong Kong Ltd
14 Lisle Street
London WC2 7BE
Tel: 020 7437 0014

Hong Kong Supermarket
62 High Street
London SW4 7UL
Tel: 020 7720 2069

Loon Fung Supermarket
42–44 Gerrard Street
London W1V 7LP
Tel: 020 7437 7332

New Peking Supermarket
59 Westbourne Grove
London W2 4UA
Tel: 020 7928 8770

Newport Supermarket
28–29 Newport Court
London WC2H 7PQ
Tel: 020 7437 2386

Rum Wong Supermarket
London Road
Guildford
Surrey GU1 2AF
Tel: 01483 451 568

S. W. Trading Ltd
Horn Lane
Greenwich
London SE10 0RT
Tel: 020 8293 9393

Wang Thai Supermarket
101 Kew Road
Richmond
Surrey TW9 2PN
Tel: 020 8332 2959

The Wing On Department
  Store (Hong Kong) Ltd
37–38 Margaret Street
London W1N 7FA
Tel: 020 7580 3677

Wing Tai
11a Aylesham Centre
Rye Lane
London SE15 5EW
Tel: 020 7635 0714

Wing Yip
395 Edgware Road
London NW2 6LN
Tel: 020 7450 0422

also at
Oldham Road
Ancoats
Manchester
M4 5HU
Tel: 0161 832 3215

and
375 Nechells Park Road
Nechells
Birmingham
B7 5NT
Tel: 0121 327 3838

South-east Asian

Hopewell Emporium
2f Dyne Road
London NW6 7XB
Tel: 020 7624 5473

Manila Supermarket
11–12 Hogarth Place
London SW5 0QT
Tel: 020 7373 8305

Miah, A. and Co
20 Magdalen Street
Norwich NR3 1HE
Tel: 01603 615395

Sri Thai
56 Shepherd's Bush Road
London W6 7PH
Tel: 020 7602 0621

Talad Thai Ltd
320 Upper Richmond Road
London SW15 6TL
Tel: 020 8789 8084

Tawana
18–20 Chepstow Road
London W2 5BD
Tel: 020 7221 6316

Japanese

Arigato
48–50 Brewer Street
London W1R 3HM
Tel: 020 7287 1722

Miura Japanese Foods
44 Coombe Road
Nr Kingston KT2 7AF
Tel: 020 8549 8076

also at
5 Limpsfield Road
Sanderstead
Surrey CR2 9LA
Tel: 020 8651 4498

Natural House
Japan Centre
212 Piccadilly
London W1V 9LD
Tel: 020 7434 4218

Oriental City
399 Edgware Road
London NW9 0JJ
Tel: 020 8200 0009

T.K. Trading
Unit 6/7
The Chase Centre
Chase Road
London NW10 6QD
Tel: 020 8453 1001

Thai

Rum Wong Supermarket
London Road
Guildford
Surrey GU1 2AF
Tel: 01483 451568

Talad Thai Ltd
320 Upper Richmond Road
London SW15 6TL
Tel: 020 8789 8084

Tawana Supermarket
18 Chepstow Road
London W2 4BD
Tel: 020 7221 6316

Equipment

Neal Street East
5–7 Neal Street
London WC2 9PV
Tel: 020 7240 0135

Obhrai Cash and Carry
168 Ealing Road
Wembley
Middlesex HA0 4DQ
Tel: 020 8903 4450

Popat Store
138 Ealing Road
Wembley
Middlesex HA0 4PY
Tel: 020 8903 6797

Mail Order Companies

Fiddes Payne Herbs and
  Spices Ltd
Unit 3B, Thorpe Way
Banbury
Oxfordshire OX16 8XL
Tel: 01295 253 888

Fox's Spices
Mason's Road
Stratford-upon-Avon
Warwickshire CV37 9XN
Tel: 01789 266 420

General Information

Bart's Spices
York Road
Bedminster
Bristol BS3 4AD
Tel: 0117 977 3474
Fax: 0117 972 0216

Fiddes Payne Herbs and
  Spices Ltd
Unit 3B, Thorpe Way
Banbury
Oxfordshire OX16 8XL
Tel: 01295 253 888

Sharwood's Ethnic
  Food Bureau
Nexus Choat
Bury House
126–128 Cromwell Road
London SW7 4ET
Tel: 020 7373 4537

AUSTRALIA

Asian Supermarkets
Pty Ltd
116 Charters Towers Road
Townsville
QLD 4810
Tel: (07) 4772 3997
Fax: (07) 4771 3919

PK Supermarkets Pty Ltd
369 Victoria Avenue
Chatswood
NSW 2067
Tel: (02) 9419 8822

Kongs Trading Pty Ltd
8 Kingscote Street
Kewdale
WA 6105
Tel: (08) 9353 3380
Fax: (08) 9353 3390

Duc Hung Long Asian
  Foodstore
95 The Crescent
Fairfield
NSW 2165
Tel: (02) 9728 1092

Exotic Asian Groceries
  Q Supercentre
Cnr Market and Bermuda
  Streets
Mermaid Waters
QLD 4218
Tel: (07) 5572 8188

Saigon Asian Food Retail
  and Wholesale
6 Cape Street
Dickson
ACT 2602
Tel: (02) 6247 4251

The Spice and Herb
  Asian Shop
200 Old Cleveland Road
Capalaba
QLD 4157
Tel: (07) 3245 5300

Sydney Fish Market Pty Ltd
Cnr Pyrmont Bridge Road and
  Bank Street
Pyrmont
NSW 2009
Tel: (02) 9660 1611

Harris Farm Markets
Sydney Markets
Flemongton
NSW 2140
Tel: (02) 9746 2055
(Also in QLD, plus
suburban stores)

Burlington Supermarkets
Chinatown Mall
Fortitude Valley
QLD 4006
Tel: (07) 3216 1828

Author's Acknowledgements

Sallie Morris would like
to thank her family:
Johnnie, Alex and James
for their support and
Beryl Castles for her
help in typing the
manuscript.

Deh-ta Hsiung would like
to thank Sallie Morris for
her advice and help in
writing about South-east
Asian foods and Emi
Kazuko for her advice
and help in writing about
Japanese products.

INDEX

**Picture
Acknowledgements**

All pictures are by Nicki
Dowie and Janine
Hosegood, except:
p8, Tony Stone/Glen
Allison, Cephas/Nigel
Blythe; p9 Cephas/Alain
Proust, Cephas/Nigel
Blythe; p10 Tony
Stone/Ron Dahlquist.

NOTES

NOTES

NOTES